DARKROOM TECHNIQUES

Vol. 2

Equipment Materials

Contact Printing

Enlarging

by Andreas Feininger

PRENTICE-HALL, INC.

ENGLEWOOD CLIFFS, N.J.

Second Revised Printing 1976

Copyright©1974 by Andreas Feininger

Published in Garden City, N.Y., by American Photographic Book Publishing
Co., Inc. All rights reserved. No part of this book may be reproduced in any
form or by any means without the written consent of the publisher.

Library of Congress Catalog No. 73-82108

ISBN 0-8174-0563-1

Manufactured in the United States of America.

Other books by ANDREAS FEININGER

Roots of Art (1975)
The Perfect Photograph (1974)
Photographic Seeing (1973)
Principles of Composition in Photography (1973)
Shells (1972)
Basic Color Photography (1972)
Total Picture Control (1970)
The Color Photo Book (1969)
Trees (1968)
Forms of Nature and Life (1966)
The Complete Photographer (1965)
New York (1964)
The World Through My Eyes (1963)
Maids, Madonnas and Witches (1961)
Man and Stone (1961)
The Anatomy of Nature (1956)
Changing America (1955)
The Creative Photographer (1955)
Successful Color Photography (1954)
Successful Photography (1954)
The Face of New York (1954)
Advanced Photography (1952)
Feininger on Photography (1949)
New York (1945)
New Paths in Photography (1939)

Table of Contents

I. Preliminaries

A word about this book

This is Volume II of a two-part series on darkroom techniques, the first part of which was devoted to *The Darkroom, Film Development,* and *Photochemistry*. Dividing a complex subject like this into two parts has both advantages and disadvantages. A reader wishing to know more about, say, the specific aspects of contact printing or enlarging does not have to buy a book on film development, a subject in which he may not be interested since he lets a commercial photofinisher do this job. Someone living on a limited budget may be loath to spend a relatively large amount on a one-volume book on darkroom techniques but may be able to afford two smaller, less expensive volumes, one at a time.

The disadvantage of a two-volume presentation is, of course, the fact that, to some extent, film development and printmaking require the same facilities and equipment and are subject to the same prerequisites and rules. Consequently, in a two-part series, ideally, these should be discussed in both books. This, however, would be unfair to the reader who buys both volumes and sees no reason why he should pay for the same information twice. The best way of solving this dilemma seemed to me to compromise: On the following pages, I give a brief synopsis of those chapters of Volume I that deal with the darkroom and other factors common to both film development and printmaking, enough to enable the reader to make contact prints and enlargements without recourse to Volume I. Should he later feel the need for more specific information, he will find the answers in the respective chapters of Volume I.

WHY A PHOTOGRAPHER SHOULD PRINT HIS OWN NEGATIVES

Making your own contact prints and enlargements gives you the following advantages over your less enterprising colleagues:

Quality and Control. The average commercial print is made by a computerized machine that analyzes the negative sensitometrically and then sets the printing controls to produce a print of *average* contrast and density. If your photographs are average, this will probably result in acceptable prints. However, if they are not, the product will be a total disappointment. Shots taken in the rain or fog will turn out too contrasty or, conversely, backlighted scenes will appear too gray. In other words, the special quality of the subject, which made you take the picture in the first place, would be missing in the photograph because the machine didn't know what you had in mind and therefore could not express your vision in picture form. Only you, the photographer, the creator of your pictures, can do this.

Experimentation. On the basis of sensitometrically established data, your photofinisher will present you with a single print of your negative. In contrast, in your own darkroom, you can make any number of prints from the same negative, all slightly different in contrast, lightness or darkness, manner of cropping, proportions, size, and so on. In other words, you can experiment to your heart's desire and really go to town on the negative, exploring it in depth and extracting from it the best possible print.

Learning. The only way to become a good photographer is through practice. Reading about phototechnique and studying the work of other photographers is certainly an important part of the learning process, but it will never make you an accomplished photographer, unless you augment it by actual photographic work. Again and again, I have met and talked to photographers whose theoretical knowledge was encyclopedic but whose pictures were less than adequate. They talked too much and did too little to be able to produce quality work. Access to a darkroom with its opportunity for unlimited practicing and experimenting will provide you with an invaluable opportunity for learning. Actually, every mistake you make can be a blessing in disguise, a priceless chance to learn something new. And once a mistake is made and its cause understood, you never have to make the same mistake again.

Stimulation. Any good photograph is the result of a successful synthesis of art and technique. Accordingly, the need for learning does not apply solely to phototechnical aspects, but also to artistic considerations: Should a print be lighter or darker, more or less contrasty, cropped to proportions that are different from those of the film, or perhaps be presented in the form of a sectional enlargement of the negative in order to improve the composition? These are questions that can only be answered by the photographer himself, preferably in the stimulating atmosphere of his own darkroom, where solitude and quiet are conducive to contemplation; where in semi-darkness enhanced by pools of amber light the mind feels free from the pressure of daily life and able to concentrate on the creation of the picture; where inspired thoughts and ideas can be translated immediately and without loss of spontaneity into actual prints.

Monetary savings. Over the years, despite the cost of the initial investment and the running charges, making your own prints is ever so much cheaper than letting a commercial photofinisher do the job.

PREREQUISITES FOR SUCCESS

Sometimes, a cause is completely out of proportion to its effect. In photography, this happens to be the case in regard to the following deceptively simple "rules," disregarding of which can take all the pleasure out of picture-making:

Make cleanliness a fetish. Nothing is more discouraging than spending hours of work and care (not to mention the cost of the material) on making pictures, only to emerge from the darkroom with spotty prints. To avoid this possibility, a photographer must know how to deal with the cause of spots in prints, which is twofold: dust and chemical contamination.

Dust settling on negatives manifests itself in the form of white dots or wiggly lines in the print. To avoid these, subject your entire darkroom to periodic, thorough cleanings with a vacuum cleaner, including the shelves, the moldings (if present), the top of the lamps, and the outside and *inside* of the enlarger. Avoid the use of lint-producing clothing, towels, and materials such as paper towels, and, above all, *do not smoke in the darkroom!*

Chemical contamination manifests itself primarily in the form of brown or yellow stains. Chemically contaminated solutions produce spotty or streaky prints, work less efficiently, or do not work at all. Particularly sensitive in this respect are developers, which can be ruined by traces of stop bath or fixer solution. To minimize the danger of chemical contamination, do not fill processing trays so high that there is danger of spilling; avoid splashing; immediately wipe up accidentally spilled processing solutions before they can dry, crystallize, become airborne in the form of dust, settle on negatives and sensitized papers, and contaminate the entire darkroom. Do not manipulate prints in the processing trays with your hands but use print tongs—one pair of tongs for the developer, another pair for stop bath and fixer—and never let the developer tongs come in contact with other solutions. If this happens accidentally, rinse the tongs briefly before using them again. Keep hands and fingers dry: A towel is a vital necessity in any darkroom. Touching the emulsion side of sensitized paper with damp hands, whether chemically contaminated or not, results in the appearance of indelible fingermarks in the print. All processing equipment should be washed at the end of each working session and used towels replaced frequently with freshly laundered ones.

Be well organized. The best insurance against mishaps due to forgetfulness, mixups, unfamiliarity, and so on is routine. Accordingly, follow basic instructions, establish a system of doing things, then stick to it, always performing the same operation in the same manner. Keep each piece of darkroom equipment in its appointed place where it is handy, yet safe from dust and chemical contamination. Make sure that bottles and containers are properly identified and clearly labelled; if necessary, make your own labels by cutting them from inch-wide, white surgical tape and writing on them with a permanent ink marker or a ballpoint pen. Keep a pencil and a writing pad or clipboard handy to jot down material in short supply, ideas that occur to you while at work, technical data pertaining to exposure, dodging, and so on. The more highly organized your routine, the less thought has to be wasted on trivia and the more time and interest can be given to that aspect of printmaking that matters most, the creation of the picture.

Read and follow instructions. Except for simple items like trays, funnels, and graduates, every piece of darkroom equipment, every bottle or can of developer, fixer, or hypo-neutralizer, every package of sensitized paper is accompanied by instructions for use. I cannot urge the reader strongly enough to read these instructions carefully and follow them to the letter, at least in the beginning. They were compiled by the manufacturer of the product to help the user get the most out of it—and believe me, nobody knows more about a product than its manufacturer, nor has anybody a greater interest in its successful acceptance than the manufacturer who wants the user to be satisfied, come back, and buy more. As far as specific products are concerned—whether an enlarger, a safelight, a developer, a sensitized paper of specific make—these are *the only specific instructions* a photographer ever needs. And since they *always* accompany the product and are *free*, no *specific* instructions for use will be given in this book, thereby avoiding a fault of many photographic textbooks that contain specific instructions galore heedless of the fact that, sooner or later, they will become useless, obsolete, and superseded by new ones because manufacturers constantly improve their products. There is, therefore, no need for the reader to worry whether or not the instructions he just read are still valid.

False economy, carelessness, and forgetfulness are the three greatest obstacles to satisfactory darkroom work. Common examples of *false economy* are efforts on the part of the photographer to save money by buying cheap unknown brands of chemicals or sensitized paper, or outdated paper by well-known manufacturers at temptingly low prices; using an inexpensive, colored lightbulb instead of a more expensive but ever so much safer, filter-equipped safelight; and overworking processing solutions despite the facts that chemicals are just about the cheapest items in the photographic budget and that exhausted solutions invariably produce impermanent or stained prints. *Carelessness* manifests itself in spilled solutions (which can lead to chemical contamination of the entire darkroom), fingermarks on negatives and prints, unlabelled bottles and containers leading to disastrous mixups, and using the fingers instead of print tongs—perhaps the commonest cause of stained prints. And a common, yet catastrophic example of *forgetfulness* is failure to close the box or envelope of unexposed sensitized paper before turning on the white light, thereby irrevocably ruining the entire paper supply.

THE DARKROOM

Since photographic papers are considerably less sensitive to light than films, the requirements in regard to lighttightness are less severe for a darkroom intended solely for printing than for one intended for film development. Photographers who let a photo store or commercial photofinisher develop their films can take advantage of this fact by setting up their equipment in any ordinary room after dark, when black makeshift drapes in front of windows are sufficient to keep out stray light from street lamps, automobile headlights, and neighboring buildings.

As far as choosing the location for such an improvised darkroom is concerned, the following considerations might help:

The kitchen is normally the most suitable room for an apartment dweller because it has the following assets: electric outlet, running water, a sink with drain, and a waterproof working surface large enough to accommodate the enlarger and the processing trays. Finished prints can be washed right on the spot. The disadvantage, which it shares with most other improvised darkroom installations, is, of course, that it can be used only when not required for its original purpose. Normally, this means working at night; on the other hand, this simplifies the window-darkening operation.

An ordinary room, because it lacks running water and a sink, is a less practical darkroom substitute than the kitchen, but it has the advantage of greater privacy and availability for longer and more convenient periods of time. A deep tray filled with water accommodates finished prints until they can be washed in the bathroom. A thick layer of newspapers over a large sheet of plastic protects the working surface from damage due to accidentally spilled solutions—a possibility that experienced photographers minimize by using extra-deep trays for fixer and water and by not filling a shallow developer tray too full.

The bathroom is normally the least desirable location for a temporary darkroom setup because the worker is never safe from interruption by other members of the household, unless, of course, a second bathroom or toilet exist. If there is no space for a table, a sheet of plywood placed over the tub provides the working surface but must be raised sufficiently to make working conditions tolerable. And even if cabinet space is available, the enlarger, chemicals, and photographic paper must never be stored in a bathroom because dampness would ruin them in a relatively short time.

A walk-in closet of the kind usually found only in older homes, if 5′ x 5′ or larger, can be converted into a small but workable darkroom. A light-tight darkroom fan installed above the door provides for ventilation. Finished prints can be washed later in the bathroom.

A corner in the basement of a private home can usually be partitioned off and turned into a first-class permanent darkroom. It has these advantages: freedom from interruption, plenty of space, availability of electricity and running water, and relatively even temperature all year round.

The attic of a private home, although offering seclusion and space, often has serious drawbacks: It is too cold in winter (unless heated, perhaps by means of a portable electric heater), and too hot in summer (unless air-conditioned), and running water is usually not available on the same floor.

Test for lighttightness

After finishing your makeshift darkroom installation but before attempting your first print, check the adequacy of your darkening arrangement by making the following test: With *all* lights turned off, place a small piece of photographic paper, emulsion side up, on your work table and put a few coins on it. Leave it exposed like that for five minutes, then develop and fix it in total darkness. If this test strip comes out pure white, whatever stray light may be present is harmless as far as this type of paper is concerned. But if the positions of the coins reveal themselves in the form of white circles on a faintly (or not so faintly) gray background, the amount of stray light present is too high and the darkening arrangement needs improving.

Complete information on darkroom installation and organization can be found in Volume I of *Darkroom Techniques.*

II. Equipment and material

The following "shopping list" is intended as a guide to photographers who are ready to furnish their first darkroom for printmaking. It contains only items that, in my opinion, are indispensable for the satisfactory production of black-and-white prints. Some of this equipment, of course, is similar or identical to that required for film development. Subsequently, each item mentioned in this checklist will be discussed in some detail.

The equipment for printmaking

Safelight	Print tongs	Paper-trimmer
Contact printer	Print-washer	Negative punch
Enlarger	Print-drier	Watercolor brushes
Paper easel	Paper safe	Tacking iron
Trays	Focusing magnifier	Dry-mounting press
Graduates	Camel's-hair brush	Apron
Bottles	Syringe	Towel
Funnels	Dodgers	Waste can
Stirring rods	Print roller	

The material for printmaking

Sensitized paper	Viscose sponges	Dry-mounting tissue
Paper developer	Absorbent cotton	Print-spotting colors
Acid stop bath	Tape	Pencil and paper
Fixer or hypo	White petroleum jelly	Felt-tipped permanent
Hypo-neutralizer	or Scratch-Patch	ink marker
Ferricyanide	Kerodex 71 protective	
	hand cream	

THE EQUIPMENT

Equipment is our capital investment, the tools of our craft which, hopefully, will be used for years to come. Photographers who take their hobby seriously are urged to stay away from cheap darkroom kits and buy instead high-quality products from a reputable photo store; if necessary, buy through the ads in photo magazines, by mail.

Safelight. The purpose of a safelight is twofold: to furnish a darkroom illumination that is *safe*, that is, gives off light of a color to which the photographic paper is insensitive yet bright enough to provide a level of illumination that enables the worker to find his way in the darkroom and judge accurately the degree of lightness or darkness of his developing prints. These conditions will be fulfilled if the photographer buys a darkroom lamp equipped with the kind of filter that the paper manufacturer specifies for his product, and then uses it in accordance with the accompanying instructions. He should pay particular attention to the maximum wattage of the lightbulb that may be used and the minimum distance from the light-sensitive material at which the safelight is still safe.

Differently sensitized photographic materials require, of course, different kinds of safelight filters. For paper processing, the following Kodak filters are recommended:

Light amber (Kodak Safelight Filter No. OC) for processing regular and polycontrast black-and-white enlarging papers and for making contact prints.

Dark amber (Kodak Safelight Filter No. 10) for processing Ektacolor and Ektachrome paper, Ektacolor print film, and Panalure paper.

Unfortunately, no safelight is safe under all conditions; its cumulative effect may eventually affect the light-sensitive emulsion, or its spectral composition may change due to gradual filter deterioration with age. Therefore, if you take your photography seriously, you may want to perform the following test:

Make sure your darkroom is free from external stray light (see the test described on p. 15), which, if present, might invalidate the test.

Place a small sheet of paper of normal contrast in the easel (which should be set for the widest possible white border to assure a reference area of pure white). Then, without a negative in the enlarger, expose it under the enlarger lamp in such a way that, after development, it will have a medium-to-light gray tone.

Place the exposed paper, emulsion side up, at the normal working distance from the safelight, but immediately cover one-quarter of it with a piece of cardboard. Expose the uncovered area to safelight illumination for one minute, then advance the cardboard until it covers half the paper. Expose the open half of the sensitized paper once more for one minute, then advance the cardboard again until it covers three-quarters of the paper. This time, expose the last quarter of the paper for two minutes, then turn the safelight off and develop the test paper in total darkness for two minutes, fix it for one minute, and examine it by white light.

Exposed as described above, the four sections of the paper received safelight exposures of no time, one minute, two minutes, and four minutes, respectively. If the safelight is safe, the first three sections should look identical in regard to gray tone, whereas the last one, which received four minutes of safelight exposure, may have a slightly darker shade. This is normal for a fast projection paper, so be warned that such papers should not be exposed unnecessarily long to safelight illumination. (Shield the developing paper from *direct* safelight exposure or develop in total darkness for the first half of the development.) If, however, strip No. 3, or strips Nos. 2 and 3, are darker than strip No. 1 (which received virtually no safelight exposure), then the safelight is not safe in use with that paper under the present working conditions. In that case, four possible causes of the observed fog must be investigated: *(1)* The safelight filter is unsuitable as far as your type of paper is concerned; *(2)* the safelight bulb is too strong; *(3)* the distance between safelight and paper is too short; *(4)* and the safelight filter has faded due to age. In each case, the remedy is obvious.

Incidentally, safelight-induced fog may not show up on the white borders of a print at all but only on areas that have been previously exposed to white light and thereby made especially sensitive (controlled pre-fogging is a well-known method of hypersensitizing film). For this reason, merely exposing a piece of paper to safelight illumination without giving it a prior exposure to white light and developing it may not reveal safelight fog, which, however, in the normal course of procedure might be strong enough to degrade the highlight areas of a print. Furthermore, photographic paper is much more sensitive to light dry than wet, its sensitivity decreasing rapidly following immersion in the developer. Shielding dry paper from unnecessary or excessive safelight exposure is therefore even more important than shielding the developing print.

Contact printer. The simplest kind of contact printer is a sheet of *quarter-inch plate glass* laid on top of the paper-plus-negative sandwich, the entire stack then being placed on the baseboard of the enlarger and exposed with the aid of its lamp (without a negative in the enlarger). The photographer can also make himself a workable contact printer by hinging a sheet of quarter-inch plate glass with surgical tape to a plywood base, placing his paper-plus-negative sandwich between the wood and glass, and exposing again under the enlarger. For more convenient handling, the glass should be about a quarter-inch wider than the base plate, which should be at least one-quarter inch thick. To avoid possible injury to the fingers, the edges of the glass should be rounded by rubbing them against a piece of sandstone or a brick. A third possibility is a printing frame of the kind available in any photo store; such frames come in all the popular paper sizes. All three devices have the advantage (especially appreciated in case of gang printing, p. 48) that they permit the photographer to correct differences in the density of his negatives by dodging or burning in (p. 97), a corrective practice not possible if a commercial *contact printer* is used. The latter is a glass-topped box containing a lightbulb activated by a switch, which lights up when a hinged platen is pressed down upon the negative-plus-paper sandwich resting on top of the glass.

Enlarger. Since the enlarger is the most expensive piece of darkroom equipment, it should be selected with particular care. Because of the large number of models available, all different in size, design, quality, and price, this may seem easier said than done. But what at first appears to be an almost overwhelming problem can be reduced to a routine operation if approached systematically step-by-step. You should pay particular attention to the following:

Quality and price. Undoubtedly, the price of the enlarger is a crucial factor. How much can a photographer afford to pay for this indispensable piece of equipment? In my opinion, however, it is less important how much he pays than the way in which he spends his money; ignorance or succumbing to snob appeal can be expensive. For example, when faced with a choice between two apparently similar enlarger models more or less identically priced, one equipped with manual and the other with automatic focusing, an inexperienced photographer would probably take the latter. However, the fact that the more complicated, automatic enlarger costs no more than the simpler, manual one would warn a more experienced buyer that the explanation of this apparent paradox must lie in a difference in the quality of the two instruments: The manual enlarger is probably of higher mechanical quality, or equipped with a better lens, than the automatic one. And since automatic focusing is at best only a convenience, but has not the slightest influence upon the quality of the print, the experienced photographer would take the manual enlarger—and get a better buy for his money.

Apart from the obvious fact that its size must fit the negative, high quality, in my experience, is the most important requirement of any enlarger—and quality is directly related to price: the better, the more expensive. Therefore, if necessary, I would rather buy a top-quality *used* enlarger in good condition than a brand-new one of lower quality if the cost of both were the same. Naturally, I would carefully inspect the used enlarger and buy only from a reputable dealer or person. Unlike automobiles, where even an economy model will get you safely from here to there although the ride may be somewhat rough, when it comes to enlargers, an economy model will usually *not* take you to your goal, the satisfactory print. Most cheap enlargers suffer from certain faults that render them inherently unfit to produce technically perfect prints; their inefficient lighting systems have hot spots, which manifest themselves in prints whose centers are darker than the edges; their poorly corrected lenses yield prints with unsharp corners; their undersized supports are super-sensitive to vibration with the result that prints are often blurred; their tinny film-holding and focusing mechanisms are easily bent out of alignment, as a result of which one side of the print might be sharp and the other unsharp. And so on. Name-dropping might be the sign of a snob, but when it comes to enlargers, it has one advantage: As long as a photographer stays clear of unknown makes, store brands, or specials and chooses only from well-known, nationally advertised name brands, he cannot really go wrong.

The size of the enlarger is determined by the size of the negatives that have to be enlarged. The three most popular sizes are 35mm, 2¼″ x 2¼″, and 4″ x 5″. Enlargers for smaller and larger negatives are, of course, also available.

Photographers who use only one film format have no problem, as far as enlarger size is concerned. But photographers who own cameras for different film formats must decide whether to acquire a convertible enlarger that can handle several negative sizes, or a separate enlarger for each. In this respect, experience has shown that, although any convertible enlarger can, at least theoretically, handle *all* film formats that are smaller than its own largest size, there are practical limits: The smallest size which, for example, a 4″ x 5″ convertible enlarger can handle efficiently is 35mm; and it is impractical to use a 5″ x 7″ enlarger for anything smaller than 4″ x 5″. In other words, photographers who own, in addition to larger cameras, say, a Minox or an Olympus Pen-FT 18 x 24mm SLR, would do well to acquire a special enlarger for these minute formats and a second, convertible enlarger to handle their other negatives up to and including 4″ x 5″. Anything larger than 4″ x 5″ should again be handled by a separate enlarger.

The three basic types of enlarger construction. Left: Vertical tubular column. *Center:* Inclined beam column. *Right:* Braced girder construction.

Enlarger construction and support. The main requirement is rigidity, resistance to deformation and vibration. The least expensive and hence most common design uses a vertical, tubular column to support the head; unfortunately, this design is also the least efficient one, because it is inherently subject to the following faults: If the base of the column is too narrow or the column itself too weak, the weight of the enlarger head will pull the column forward, upsetting the vitally important parallel alignment between negative and paper and leading to partly unsharp prints; if the support system is not sufficiently rigid, the enlarger becomes so sensitive to vibration that prints are easily blurred; if sections of a negative have to be greatly enlarged, the chrome-plated column may reflect light transmitted by the front edge of the negative onto the paper, causing flare and fog in the print (this can be avoided by proper masking of the negative, or temporarily covering the negative areas that will not be shown in the print with a frame cut out of thin black paper); and finally, if very large prints have to be made, the base of the column may get in the way of the paper easel with the result that, although the height of the column is adequate and the focal length of the lens sufficiently short, the desired degree of enlargement cannot be achieved. Enlargers whose supporting columns lean forward at an angle, particularly those which employ a massive column with a triangular cross-section, as well as most support systems that assure rigidity by means of struts and braces, avoid these faults.

The illuminating system of any enlarger consists of two parts: a lamp and a device (a condenser or a diffuser) to insure evenness of illumination at the focal plane (the paper). In accordance with the nature of these components, two basically different designs must be distinguished, each with its own characteristics:

1. *Tungsten lamp-with-condenser enlargers* are particularly suitable for enlarging black-and-white or color negatives up to and including 4 "x 5". Illumination is furnished either by a photo enlarger lamp of appropriate wattage (or, provided the lamp-house is suitably designed, a tungsten-halogen lamp) in conjunction with a single or double condenser. Photo enlarger lamps come in five sizes:

No. 211	=	75 watts	No. 213 = 250 watts	
No. 212	=	150 watts	No. 302 = 500 watts	
		No. 521 = 1000 watts		

The first three sizes are intended for use in enlargers accommodating negatives up to and including 4" x 5", the last two for use in larger instruments. Tungsten-halogen lamps have one advantage over photo enlarger lamps: Their light output remains uniform throughout the life of the lamp. (Photo enlarger lamps gradually darken with age and thereby change in regard to the spectral composition of their light, a drawback as far as color printing is concerned.) Smart photographers buy their enlarger with *two* lamps, keeping one as a spare in case the other one burns out.

2. *Fluorescent tube-with-diffuser enlargers* are particularly suited for enlarging negatives larger than 4" x 5" and for portrait work. Also known as cold-light enlargers, they differ from tungsten lamp-with-condenser enlargers in two important respects: their light is considerably softer, as a result of which negative contrast is reduced, minor blemishes and scratches in the negative tend to be less noticeable, and film grain is minimized; and they are unsuitable for use with variable-contrast papers and for color printing.

Suitability for color printing. Although basically any tungsten (or halogen) lamp-with-condenser enlarger can be used for color printing, provided it is equipped with heat-absorbing glass (Pittsburgh No. 2043) and an ultraviolet-absorbing filter (Kodak CP2B), some designs are more convenient (and also more expensive) than others. The best color enlargers are equipped with a tungsten-halogen lamp and built-in, precisely graded and calibrated, permanent color filters which can be set with the aid of three dials, one for each of the three color filter disks. Not quite as practical (but also less expensive) are those color enlargers that feature a special filter drawer for inserting the appropriate filter pack between the negative and the lamp; in this position, filter quality does not affect the sharpness of the print, as a result of which relatively inexpensive acetate (Kodak CP) filters can be used. And finally, there are the ordinary enlargers that do not feature special filter drawers and must therefore be used only in conjunction with the relatively expensive, but optically superior Color Compensating (Kodak CC) filters, which are placed in front of the lens, where filters of lesser quality would be a potential source of unsharpness.

Enlarger lenses differ in two respects from ordinary picture-taking lenses which, with the exception of certain reproduction or process-lenses, would yield less satisfactory results if they were mounted on an enlarger: Enlarger lenses are computed to give maximum sharpness at short (instead of medium-to-great) lens-to-subject (here, lens-to-paper) distances; and they have a particularly flat field, *i.e.*, they produce critical sharpness over the entire area of the print. At least, this is the theory; in practice, there are considerable differences even among genuine enlarging lenses and, not surprisingly, the good ones cost more than the mediocre ones of comparable focal length and speed. Next to suitability in regard to focal length, high quality is therefore the most important characteristic of any enlarging lens, and to skimp here is one of the surest ways to take all the joy out of dark-room work; for what is the use of buying fine, expensive cameras and putting a lot of work and money into printmaking only to end up with a fuzzy picture?

The focal length of an enlarger lens is determined by the size of the negative that has to be enlarged and should be approximately equal to the length of its diagonal; the relative aperture is usually $f/4.5$ or $f/5.6$. For best results in sharpness and evenness of light distribution, enlarger lenses should be stopped down by one to two stops; excessive stopping down, however, would yield prints that are less sharp because of diffraction phenomena and, possibly, focus shift.

Two desirable, nonoptical features of enlarging lenses that ought to be considered are easy legibility of the f/stop numbers engraved on the lens mount and the presence of click-stops. The f/stop numbers of certain enlarging lenses are very hard to read in safelight illumination, and lenses without click-stops are difficult to stop down precisely.

The negative carrier. Distinguish between two types: glass plates and glassless carriers. Each has its own characteristics.

An effective glass negative carrier can be made by joining two sheets of Anti-Newton-Ring glass with tape. Masks of different negative sizes are cut from thin, black paper.

Glass plates have the invaluable advantage that they hold even the largest negative perfectly flat in focus, making it impossible to get out-of-focus prints caused by the buckling of the negative under the influence of heat from the enlarger lamp. On the other hand, they have four surfaces to which dust and lint can cling, and they can cause Newton's rings—irregular, concentric bands of colored light representing interference patterns caused by imperfect contact between film and glass. These patterns show particularly clearly in even-toned areas of the print, are almost impossible to retouch except by airbrush, and very difficult to avoid once the conditions for their formation are present. Negative carriers made of special anti-Newton's-ring glass are available but often difficult to get.

Glassless negative carriers consist of two open metal frames between which the negative is held more or less in focus—more or less, because heat from the enlarger lamp usually makes it buckle somewhat out of the focal plane, the more so, the larger the negative and the longer it is exposed to heat. The unavoidable result, of course, is partial unsharpness of the print. On the other hand, glassless negative carriers offer no surfaces for dust to cling to and appear as spots in the print and they preclude the formation of Newton's rings. In my opinion, glassless negative carriers are superior to glass plates when it comes to enlarging 35mm negatives (where dust is a greater nuisance, and a greater likelihood, than buckling); for enlarging 2¼″ x 2¼″ negatives, it makes very little difference which type of negative carrier is used since, in this case, the good and bad features of each more or less cancel one another; and for enlarging 4″ x 5″ negatives, glass plates are definitely preferable, because, on the one hand, large negatives buckle much more severely than small ones, and, on the other hand, the degree of enlargement is usually relatively low with the result that dust spots are smaller and less objectionable in the print and more easily eliminated by retouching.

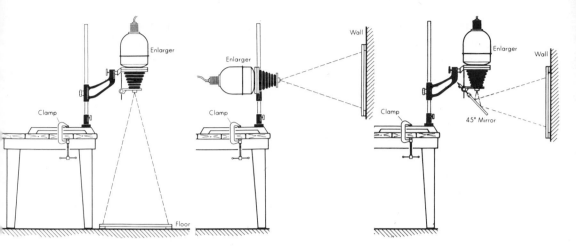

Three ways to outsized prints. Left: Swing enlarger head around the vertical column and project onto the floor, a box, chair, and the like instead of the enlarger base-board. *Center:* Swing the enlarger head around a horizontal axis and project onto the wall. *Right:* Use a 45-degree mirror or prism in front of the enlarger lens and project onto the wall.

Degree of enlargement. The degree of negative magnification of most enlargers is limited by the height of their column and the focal length of the lens: the higher the column and/or the shorter the focal length of the lens, the higher the attainable degree of enlargement. A few enlargers, however, are so constructed that still higher degrees of enlargement can be achieved by one of two means. With one type, the enlarger head can be rotated 180 degrees around a vertical axis, which makes it possible to set up the enlarger backwards, flush with the edge of the workbench. Then you can clamp its baseboard to the tabletop to prevent the instrument from toppling over the edge, rotate its head by 180 degrees, and place the paper easel on the darkroom floor or a box of suitable height instead of on the enlarger baseboard. The other type is so constructed that its head can be rotated 90 degrees around a horizontal axis, which makes it possible to project horizontally on a wall (like a projector projecting slides on a screen); the only factor limiting the degree of enlargement attainable is the length of the throw—the distance between enlarger and wall. A third possibility is to improvise by setting up a 45-degree front-surface mirror in front of the enlarger lens for horizontal projection.

Manual versus automatic focusing. The great majority of enlargers are focused by adjusting the distance between negative and lens by hand in accordance with the degree of enlargement desired while the photographer visually checks the sharpness of the print, usually with a focusing magnifier.

There are, however, a few enlargers which, by means of a coupling connecting the vertical movement of the enlarger head with the focusing movement of the lens, are always in focus, regardless of the degree of enlargement. Although, at first glance, this may seem a very desirable feature, it has certain drawbacks, the most important one being a much higher price than that of a comparable enlarger with manual focusing. Furthermore, unless the curve of the focus-guidance mechanism—the cam— is perfectly matched with the focal length of the lens, automatic focus will not be maintained throughout the entire magnification range of the enlarger. And since the *actual* focal length of a lens hardly ever coincides precisely with the rated (engraved) focal length, to insure perfect automatic focusing, the curve of the cam of each enlarger must be individually adapted to the specific lens which it will guide. In other words, lenses on automatic enlargers are not freely interchangeable (as they are with manually operated enlargers), but must be ordered from the factory at the time of purchase of the enlarger. And finally, it has been my experience that, in practice, even with matched lenses, precise focus is not always maintained and, for maximum sharpness, a final manual lens adjustment (refocusing) may be required. For these reasons, I prefer manual enlargers to automatics.

Perspective control. A feature of limited application but enormous practical value when needed is a tilting negative stage or lens mount. With their aid, a photographer can restore to the parallel lines that were parallel in the subject, but were rendered converging in the negative as a result of tilting the camera. (An example is the sides of tall buildings.) This is tantamount to correcting perspective, a possibility which will be particularly appreciated by architectural, industrial, and commercial photographers who, for reasons of convenience or due to lack of time or space, used a 35mm or 2¼″ x 2¼″ camera, when, for best results, they should have taken the picture with a swing-equipped view camera. The technique of controlling perspective with the aid of an enlarger is discussed on p. 117.

Conclusion. Choosing the most suitable enlarger on the basis of information given above should not be difficult if the reader answers the following questions one by one:

How much money can I afford to invest in an enlarger? Would I get a better buy if I bought a used instead of a new machine?

What are the nationally advertised brands of enlargers? (Ask your photo dealer, then get yourself descriptive literature and study it leisurely at home.)

Do I need a one-size or a multiple-size (convertible) enlarger? Do I want to enlarge one or several negative formats?

Are there enlargers in the price range that I can afford (and, of course, in the size I need for my films) with inclined or strut-braced columns?

What kind of illuminating system do I need?

Do I also want to enlarge color negatives and make color prints?

The lens should be no problem: I want the best.

The type of negative carrier is given, too: glassless for 35mm; doesn't matter for 2¼″ x 2¼″; anti-Newton's-ring-glass plates for 4″ x 5″.

Manual or automatic focusing?

Do I want to be able to make larger-than-normal prints? In that case, the enlarger should have a head that can be rotated around either the vertical or the horizontal axis. Alternatively, you could also use a 45-degree front-surface mirror in front of the enlarger lens for horizontal projection.

Do I need the perspective-control device?

Paper easel. Its purposes are to hold the paper flat in the plane of focus and to provide for a white border around the print. Choose between two types: fixed and adjustable. Fixed paper easels, which are relatively inexpensive, resemble picture frames without glass and come in all the standard paper sizes up to 11″ x 14″, but each frame takes only one size of paper. Adjustable easels accept paper in their own as well as in any smaller size, and, within their size range, enable a photographer to make prints in any rectangular shape desired from square to extremely narrow. The most useful easel size is 11″ x 14″.

Trays for processing solutions come in many different sizes and materials. Experience has shown that trays smaller than 8″ x 10″ are all but useless for print processing, even if smaller paper sizes are involved. For the processing of larger prints, of course, the tray size must be chosen accordingly. Trays for developer and short stop solutions should be relatively shallow; fixer, hypo-eliminator, and water trays should be deep.

The two most suitable materials for processing trays are stainless steel and white, high-impact plastic, their main differences being in price and heat-conductivity: Stainless steel is much more expensive than plastic, but it lasts indefinitely and is also a better conductor of heat (which is not necessarily an advantage). Enamelled steel trays chip and rust and then become useless—a total waste of money.

Printmakers need a separate tray for each of the following processing solutions: developer, acid stop bath, first fixer, second fixer, hypo-neutralizing bath and, preferably, water for holding finished prints until they can be transferred to the print washer.

Graduates are the same as for film development. I use three: a one-gallon stainless-steel graduate for dissolving chemicals; a 500cc tapered plastic one for measuring quantities of developer; and a 50cc glass cylindrical one for precisely measuring small amounts of liquid.

Bottles are needed for storing processing solutions. Their number and sizes depend on the individual requirements of the photographer. I use plastic (polyethylene) bottles with plastic screw tops. For practical reasons, many small bottles are preferable to one or a few large ones because, in this way, prepared developer stock solutions can be stored in such a way that withdrawal for use affects only one bottle at a time, leaving the rest undisturbed in bottles filled all the way to the top, safe from contact with air, which would gradually oxidize and break down the developer.

Funnels are needed to pour freshly mixed or used processing solutions into storage bottles. I use a large stainless steel and a small plastic one.

Stirring rods are needed to stir dissolving chemicals when preparing processing solutions. I like glass rods best.

Print tongs are necessary for agitating prints in the processing solutions and transferring them from one tray to the next. A minimum of two pairs are needed: one for handling prints during development and transferring them from the developer to the short stop bath; the other to agitate the print in the short stop bath and subsequently transfer it first to the fixer and then to the hypo-eliminator. Since short stop and fixing solutions are poison as far as the developer is concerned, the tongs used for handling prints in the developer should not come in contact with these solutions, a risk that is particularly acute at the moment of transfer from the developer to the short stop tray. Should the developer tongs accidentally touch the short stop solution, they must be rinsed under running water before they can be used again.

I prefer print tongs of heavy-gauge stainless steel, the tips of which I cover with short lengths of thin rubber hose to avoid scratching the paper emulsion. Inexpensive stainless steel tongs are flimsy and bend easily; tongs made of bamboo absorb chemicals and should be avoided.

Print-washer. The most popular method of washing prints is by means of a syphon device, hooked to the edge of a deep tray standing in the sink, which is constantly replenished by a stream of running water. If necessary, to provide clearance for the exhaust spout, the tray can be placed on bricks or blocks of wood. However, in my opinion, a better way of washing prints is with the aid of the home-made print-washing tank illustrated in Vol. I. Still more efficient are large print-washers consisting of a perforated stainless steel drum that contains the prints, immersed and rotating in a deep, water-filled trough, where they are continuously agitated by a stream of fresh water; unfortunately, this kind of washer is both expensive and big.

Print-drier. Two simple and inexpensive print-drying devices are the blotter book and the blotter roll. Much more efficient are electric print-driers, which are available in a number of different designs and sizes. If prints on glossy paper should be finished with a mirror-like surface, they must be dried on *ferrotype plates*, either in the open air (which takes time) or on an electric flatbed drier. Electric drum driers permit the photographer to give prints a high-gloss finish without the aid of ferrotype plates, the drum itself having the required kind of surface.

Paper safe. This is a light-proof storage cabinet with shelves in which photographic paper can safely be stored without its lighttight wrapping— a great convenience in any darkroom.

Focusing magnifier. A common cause of slightly fuzzy enlargements is sloppy focusing on the part of the photographer. To insure grain-sharp prints—prints that are so sharp that the grain of the negative itself becomes visible—I always focus my enlarger with the aid of a focusing magnifier. This device is particularly useful in cases in which the negative is either abnormally dense, or deficient in contrast or sharply-defined detail, therefore offering the unaided eye nothing on which to focus. Best, in my opinion, but also somewhat more difficult to use, are those focusing magnifiers that work on the aerial-image principle and focus not on image detail, but directly on the film grain.

A camel's-hair brush is indispensable for cleaning negatives of loose dust particles before they are placed in the enlarger. The so-called anti-static brushes contain a polonium strip that allegedly neutralizes a negative's electrostatic charge, the force that attracts dust. An anti-static cleaner and an anti-static wipe-cloth are likewise useful aids in a darkroom.

A syringe, a rubber ball with a nozzle which sometimes is fitted with a little brush, is a handy gadget to blow dust off a negative. Blowing has the advantage over brushing or wiping that it does not charge the negative electrically. Some photographers prefer the use of canned air—ordinary air under pressure in a spray-can—for blowing dust off negatives and cleaning the inside of their enlargers. I have the feeling that, by stirring up dust, this method does more harm than good, and prefer to clean my enlarger with the aid of a vacuum cleaner.

Dodgers are indispensable aids in print contrast control (p. 97). Distinguish between two kinds: small pieces of cardboard (usually round or oval in different sizes) attached to a wire handle, for holding back negative areas that would otherwise appear too dark in the print; and pieces of cardboard with a hole in the center, for burning in negative areas that would otherwise appear too light in the print. Although such dodgers can be bought in most photo stores, photographers usually prefer to make their own.

A print roller is necessary to remove excess water from prints before they go on the drier or to insure that photographic paper is in perfect contact with the ferrotype plate, since matte spots would otherwise mar the mirror-like finish of the print.

Trimmer. Although strictly not a necessity (prints can also be trimmed with a single-edge razor blade in conjunction with a steel straightedge), a trimmer is a useful accessory in any darkroom. If paper or cardboard frequently has to be cut to specific lengths, marking these dimensions on the trimmer board with strips of white adhesive tape facilitates this operation by providing guides that can not only be seen more clearly in semi-darkness than the trimmer scale, but also be felt and used as stops against which to place the paper. Many photographers make the mistake of buying a trimmer that is too small; in my experience, a cutting edge of 16 inches is most practical for average darkroom purposes.

Negative punch. The best way of filing 35mm and roll-film negatives is to cut the film into strips containing a certain number of individual negatives called frames—three or four in the case of 2¼" x 2¼" negatives, six or seven in the case of 35mm film. Normally, of course, not all the negatives on one strip are worth enlarging, and you will want to mark those that should be printed. The simplest way to do this is to apply a dash of ink to the clear edge of the selected frame with a felt-tipped permanent ink marker. A more professional solution, however, is to punch a semi-circular piece of film out of the clear edge of the strip with a negatvie punch, producing a mark that can easily be felt in the dark. This kind of punch is similar to a railroad conductor's ticket punch. I use the Punch-Rite No. 45 N, made by P. J. Mieth Mfg. Co. in Kenilworth, N. J., which is available at better office equipment stores.

Fine watercolor brushes are needed for spotting prints. I use three brushes side by side: one for black or very dark gray, one for white, and one for intermediary shades.

Tacking iron. This is a small, electrically heated iron, which considerably facilitates the dry-mounting process. It is used to join print, dry-mounting tissue, and cardboard mount lightly together before the entire sandwich goes into the dry-mounting press for final bonding.

Dry-mounting press. Although expensive and not strictly necessary because prints can also be dry-mounted with the aid of an ordinary household flatiron, a dry-mounting press enormously facilitates this operation and usually produces more professional-looking results.

Apron. If permitted to come in contact with clothing, many photographic processing solutions produce indelible stains. A plastic darkroom apron prevents this. Kodak makes a very good one. Wearing a laboratory technician's white or beige smock may look more elegant, but it is less efficient because its fabric is easily penetrated by chemical solutions.

A towel is a vital necessity in any darkroom, since wet hands produce indelible stains on sensitized paper and permanently mark negatives. I use three: One is draped over the drawstrings of my darkroom apron and thus always handy; another one hangs near the washing tank; and a third is kept in reserve in case one of the others gets too wet. To prevent gradual chemical contamination, used towels should be replaced frequently with freshly laundered ones. A roll of paper towel would also do, but it is a producer of lint—and lint is a dirty word in any darkroom worker's vocabulary.

Waste can. A large, plastic can is an important factor in keeping a darkroom clean. Where else would you put all those under- and overexposed prints, empty developer cans, fixer bottles, and so on?

THE MATERIAL

Material means consumables—things that get used up during processing.

Sensitized paper

A very large selection of photographic papers with different chemical, physical, and visual properties are at the disposal of any photographer discriminating enough not to be satisfied with just any print. All the resulting differences in appearance, however, are only variations and combinations of a few basic qualities common to *all* photographic papers:

> **Emulsion speed**
> **Contrast gradient**
> **Paper surface**
> **Paper base**
> **Base tint**

Emulsion speed. Like films, photographic papers are manufactured with different degrees of light-sensitivity, or speed. The reason for this is that papers for different purposes require different speeds to insure manageable exposure times, *i.e.*, exposures neither so short that they become too difficult to time accurately, nor so long that they become unreasonable, causing enlargers to overheat and negatives to buckle out of focus.

The speed of photographic papers is expressed in ANSI Paper Speed numbers which are computed in such a way that the difference between two consecutive numbers represents an exposure change of one-third f/stop. Therefore, any difference of three intervals, say, from 64 to 125, represents an exposure difference of one full f/stop. The full range of these paper speeds (which for most Kodak papers are listed in the Kodak Data Book G-1) is as follows:

1 – 1.2 – 1.6 – 2 – 2.5 – 3 – 4 – 5 – 6 – 8 – 10 – 12 – 16 – 20 – 25 – 32 – 40 – 50 – 64 – 80 – 100 – 125 – 160 – 200 – 250 – 320 – 400 – 500 – 650 – 800 – 1000

The practical value of ANSI Paper Speed numbers is twofold:

1. They facilitate selection of a paper of proper speed. For example, in contact printing (p. 44), best results are normally achieved with a paper of relatively slow speed (like Kodak Velox, which, in No. 2 grade, has an ANSI speed of 8). For enlarging 4″ x 5″ negatives to average print sizes, a medium-fast paper usually gives the best results (like Kodak Polycontrast paper, which, in conjunction with a PC2 filter has an ANSI speed of 160). And for enlarging 35mm negatives, which require higher degrees of magnification (exposure is proportional to the square of the magnification), a relatively fast paper usually gives the best results (like Kodak Kodabromide paper, which, in No. 2 grade, has an ANSI speed of 500).

2. ANSI speeds are very handy if a photographer wants to switch from one kind of paper to another, or from one gradation to another within the same paper family. He will get approximately the same kind of print on the new type of paper, if he multiplies the known exposure—the one that gave him the best print on the first type of paper—by the speed number of this paper, and subsequently divides the result by the speed number of the second type of paper—the paper he intends to use.

Basically, slow papers (ANSI numbers 2 to 50) are best for making contact prints and for enlarging abnormally thin negatives (faster papers, of course, can also be used if the illumination is reduced accordingly); medium-fast papers (ANSI numbers 64 to 250) are best for enlarging 2¼″ x 2¼″ and larger negatives of normal densities up to ten times linear; and fast papers (ANSI speeds higher than 250) are most suitable for enlarging 35mm negatives and negatives of any size that are abnormally dense, or black.

Contrast gradient (gradation). Unfortunately, not all negatives are satisfactory in contrast range: In some, contrast is too high, in others, too low. Therefore, if the gradation, or contrast gradient, of all papers were the same, negatives of the first kind would yield prints that would look unnaturally harsh, consisting mostly of areas of black and white. On the other hand, negatives of the latter type would yield prints that would appear unnaturally flat or soft, consisting entirely of shades of medium gray. Such negative deficiencies can usually be corrected in the print with the aid of a paper of the appropriate gradation.

Gradation is the measure of the response of a photographic emulsion to contrast: A paper of normal gradation yields prints in which contrast is more or less the same as in the negative and is, therefore, most suited for printing negatives in which contrast is already satisfactory. A paper of soft gradation yields prints whose contrast is lower than in the negative and is, therefore, most suited for printing negatives whose contrast is too high. And a paper of hard gradation yields prints in which contrast is higher than in the negative and is therefore most suited for printing negatives in which contrast is too low.

Most photographic papers are made in different contrast grades identified by numbers: No. 1 represents a soft paper, which considerably reduces negative contrast in the print; No. 2 represents a normal paper, which slightly reduces negative contrast in the print; No. 3 represents a medium paper, which more or less preserves negative contrast in the print; No. 4 represents a hard paper, which increases negative contrast in the print; and No. 5 represents an extra-hard paper, which increases negative contrast in the print even more than paper No. 4. Unfortunately, however, different manufacturers apply different standards, as a result of which, for example, the No. 2 paper of one manufacturer may have a somewhat different gradation from the No. 2 paper of another, and so on. Only knowledge of a paper family's gradation range derived from tests can assure a photographer that the paper he selects for printing a specific negative is predictable, as far as contrast rendition is concerned.

Paper surface. The large number of different surfaces in which photographic papers are manufactured is likely to confuse the beginner, unless he selects his paper on the basis of the principle that the paper surface must fit the nature of the depicted subject and the size and purpose of the print. In this respect, he should consider the following:

Paper surfaces differ in two respects: texture and degree of gloss, or sheen. As far as texture is concerned, papers vary from very smooth to very rough—from the mirror-like smoothness of a ferrotyped glossy paper to the coarse and irregular surface texture of papers imprinted with designs imitating heavy sketching paper or canvas. And the degree of glossiness can vary from the polished sheen of ferrotyped glossy paper to the almost complete absence of gloss of a dead matte paper. Texture and gloss, however, are not mutually exclusive; smooth, textureless papers can have a matte surface, and textured ones can have a sheen.

As far as the relationship between paper surface, nature of the subject, and size and purpose of the print is concerned, experience has shown that in cases in which the longest possible scale of gray tones, the richest gradation, relatively high contrast, and maximum sharpness and definition are desirable, best results are always achieved if the print is made on a paper with a smooth, textureless, glossy surface, particularly if it was ferrotyped (p. 63); prints intended for reproduction in magazines, newspapers, and books should therefore always be made on glossy paper. On the other hand, prints intended for exhibition are best made on paper with a semi-matte or matte surface, which minimizes reflections—a common source of annoyance at exhibitions. In cases in which fine detail is undesirable, as sometimes in portraiture, a matte, roughly textured paper surface will probably be most satisfactory. Small prints, as a rule, look better (and sharper!) on smooth papers than on rough ones. The larger the print, the coarser the surface texture it can take. Photographers must not, however, forget to take into consideration the fact that all matte papers appear somewhat lighter and more brilliant as long as they are wet; after drying, a print that seemed just right in the developer will often be found lusterless and too dark. This is a characteristic of all matte papers for which allowance must be made during printing.

Apart from these few rules derived from experience, selection of a paper surface is strictly a matter of personal preference, although as so often when taste is concerned, restraint and simplicity are never wrong. To facilitate selection, many photo stores display the papers of different manufacturers in the form of sample-books from which a photographer can choose. I print *all* my negatives on glossy paper, ferrotyping those prints that are intended for reproduction, drying those intended for viewing or exhibiting with their emulsion side facing the canvas (instead of the ferrotype plate) of the drier to give them a semi-glossy finish.

Paper base. Most types of photographic paper are made in different degrees of thickness, called "weight." Kodak distinguishes four weights of paper stock: light-weight papers, intended for all purposes that require thinness and lightness; single-weight papers (abbreviated SW) intended for general use, provided the print size does not exceed 8″ x 10″, and for most prints regardless of size intended for mounting on cardboard; medium-weight papers, used only for special purposes like continuous processing; and double-weight papers (abbreviated DW), most suitable for unmounted prints larger than 8″ x 10″, and *all* unmounted prints regardless of size that will be subject to frequent handling.

As far as the average amateur is concerned, the choice is between SW and DW papers. Of these, SW papers are somewhat less expensive, wash and dry more rapidly, are easier to mount on cardboards, and use less filing space than DW papers. On the other hand, DW papers do not curl as easily, are less subject to buckling and warping, make a more substantial impression on the viewer or customer, and stand up better under rough treatment, such as frequent handling and filing.

Base tint. The tint or overall tone of a photograph depends on two factors: the tint of the image, and the tint of the paper base. Image tint depends on the characteristics of the paper emulsion, the type of developer, and the time and temperature of the development and may vary from brownish, or warm, tones to neutral gray and black to blue-black, or cold, tones. Base tint—the color of the paper stock—is either pure white (cold white), warm white (a barely noticeable yellow), or cream (yellow-white). Some photographers prefer cold tints for pictures of winter and water scenes, warm tints for portraits, and neutral gray tints for photographs of average subjects. I feel that a cold white tint is most in harmony with the character of the photographic medium.

Paper designation. When asking in a photo store for a specific kind of paper, a photographer must give the salesman the following information: Number of sheets; name of manufacturer and paper; size of paper; paper surface; contrast grade; and weight of paper. To give an example, he might ask for 100 sheets of Kodak Medalist paper 8″ x 10″; white, high-luster, smooth (surface J); normal gradation (No. 2); single-weight (SW).

How to store and handle paper. Photographic papers are a relatively sensitive commodity easily damaged by faulty storing and handling. To avoid disappointment and waste, careful photographers pay attention to the following:

The main enemies of photographic emulsions are heat, humidity, and time. Light-sensitive paper, therefore, must not be stored in places where the temperature is consistently above 70° F. (attics in summer) or where they would be exposed to dampness (some basements, all bathrooms). On the other hand, excessive dryness (relative humidity below approximately 30 per cent) is equally undesirable, since it makes photographic papers brittle and difficult to handle because of excessive curl, which in turn might lead to cracks in the emulsion. And after a certain length of time, photographic papers become outdated, *i.e.*, the emulsion begins to deteriorate, loose speed and contrast, and prints made on such paper would appear fogged, flat, and too gray.

Although less frequently encountered by the amateur, other deteriorating factors are certain fumes and gases such as those given off by plastic solvents, lacquer, or paint, the chemical vapors resulting from the sulfide toning process, and the exhaust gases from internal combustion engines. Photographers who have their darkrooms in or close to a workshop or a garage should give these possibilities some thought.

Since photographic emulsions deteriorate with age, most paper wrappers show the expiration date, after which the manufacturer no longer guarantees the freshness of his product. When buying photographic paper, take a look at this date and make sure that the product you get is still fresh.

When replenishing your stock of paper, do not forget to place the new supply at the bottom of the stack to make sure that the old paper is used up before the new packages are opened.

All photographic emulsions are highly sensitive to fingermarks. Sheets of photographic paper should therefore be handled only by their edges, and hands must be kept dry and free from chemicals. Print tongs and towels (pp. 28 and 31) are indispensable aids in this area.

In the dry state, photographic papers are surprisingly brittle, especially those with glossy surfaces. Inept handling before development causes surface cracks which, however, may not become apparent until the processed paper is again dry. There is no remedy: The only way to avoid unsightly cracks on the face of a print is to handle the paper gently.

Forgetting to shut the door of the paper safe (p. 29), to place the lid on the paper box, or to return unused paper to its envelope before switching on the white light leads to instant disaster—the loss of the entire paper stock through fogging.

To avoid image degradation due to safelight fog (p. 17), avoid unnecessary or excessive safelight exposure by handling paper in such a way that, whenever possible, its back instead of its emulsion side is turned toward the safelight. Keep it in the shade cast by an object or your own body. Turn the safelight off (or away) while composing and focusing the image, exposing the paper in the enlarger, and during the first minute of the development.

When writing data on the back of an unprocessed sheet of paper, place it on a smooth, hard surface (glass or formica is excellent), use a soft lead pencil (No. 1), and write lightly; otherwise, the writing may go through the paper and show up later on the face of the print. The same precautions should, of course, be taken when writing on the back of a finished print.

Unusual printing materials. In addition to the ordinary photographic papers discussed above, other printing materials with more unusual qualities exist. Except for variable-contrast papers, these are rather specialized in character, but they offer interesting possibilities for creative work to experimentally inclined photographers. Here is a quick rundown of some Kodak printing materials, which should whet the appetite of the reader:

Variable-contrast papers combine different degrees of contrast within one paper. This characteristic has the advantage that a single boxful of paper enables a photographer to do the same variety of work as if he had at his disposal four boxes of paper in the gradations from soft to extra-hard. In practice, this is equivalent to a reduction in inventory, and has the further advantage of eliminating the need to buy seldom-needed grades of paper, which might become outdated before they can be used up. In the case of Kodak Polycontrast paper, variations in gradation are brought about by means of seven different filters, providing for seven different degrees of contrast in half-grade steps between what normally would be a No. 1 and a No. 4 paper. This is a gain of three additional gradations equivalent to the contrast numbers 1½, 2½, and 3½. The required Kodak Polycontrast filters come in two qualities: high-quality gelatin filters for use in front of the enlarger lens; and cheaper acetate filters for use in enlargers equipped with filter drawers between the negative and the lamp. Because of their color-sensitive nature, variable-contrast papers must be handled with extra care by safelight illumination selected in accordance with the manufacturer's instructions.

Kodak Panalure papers have panchromatic emulsions (they are sensitive to all colors instead, like ordinary papers, only to blue) and are designed for making high-quality black-and-white prints from color negatives (Koda-color and Ektacolor films). Because they are sensitive only to the blue component of white light, ordinary photographic papers would in such cases falsify the values of the colors of the subject as we perceive them. In contrast, Panalure papers are sensitive to all colors, and would produce black-and-white prints from color negatives in which the tonal values are more or less the same as if the subject had been photographed on panchromatic film and the negative printed on ordinary paper.

Moreover, since Panalure papers are sensitive to all colors, the brightness values of the different colors of the subject can be controlled during the transformation of color into shades of gray by means of color filters, exactly as when taking photographs on panchromatic film. For minor changes in tonal balance, a Kodak Color Compensating (CC) filter in the appropriate color and density will give the best results; for major changes, a filter of the kind used for taking black-and-white photographs should be used. Because of the high color sensitivity of Panalure papers, stringent rules apply to safe-light illumination, and the paper manufacturer's instructions must be followed implicitly.

Kodak Resisto papers have ordinary emulsions on a resin-coated, water-resistant base. They have two advantages over ordinary papers: They are dimensionally much more stable; and they require appreciably shorter processing and particularly washing and drying times, since their base absorbs water and chemical solutions to a much smaller degree than ordinary paper. Recommended processing procedures, however, must be strictly followed; otherwise excessive soaking may cause the water-resistant layer to break down and the print to assume a disagreeable, mottled effect. Kodak recommends the following processing times: Develop one minute, rinse five seconds, fix two minutes, wash four minutes; before drying, excess water should be squeegeed or sponged off. Electric driers should be set not higher than 180°F. since higher temperatures impair the dimensional stability of the paper. Despite their plastic base, prints on Resisto paper can be dry-mounted in the usual way (p. 67), provided the temperature of the dry-mounting press does not exceed 190°F.

Kodak Ektamatic SC papers for stabilization processing are variable-contrast papers (p. 37) intended for use with the Kodak Polycontrast filters, which were already discussed (p. 38). Unlike ordinary photographic papers, they already contain the necessary developing agents within their emulsion, and you can process them therefore, merely by applying an activator to the paper surface. Subsequent treatment with a stabilizing agent neutralizes the activator and converts any remaining silver salts into reasonably stable chemical compounds, which must remain in the paper. Washing the finished print would ruin it. Although this method of processing by chemical stabilization has the great advantage of reducing the time of printmaking—from the moment the paper is taken off the enlarger easel to the moment the finished print is ready for use—to approximately 15 seconds, it has the drawback that such prints are subject to relatively fast deterioration. Even when kept in the dark under advantageous storage conditions, they are likely to last for only a few months. Should this be insufficient, stabilized prints, after they have served their initial purpose, can subsequently be made as permanent as any print on ordinary paper by fixing them for 8 to 12 minutes in a fixing bath for paper, followed by a brief treatment in a hypo-elimination solution, washing, and drying as described on pp. 46, 61–62.

Kodak Ektamatic SC papers must be processed in a special Kodak processor (Model 214-K, at the time of writing), which completely eliminates the need for sinks, trays, or washing facilities and yields finished prints in 15 seconds. Although slightly damp when emerging from the processor, the prints dry within a few minutes at room temperature. The stabilization process is therefore particularly well suited in cases where speed of production is essential, or where conditions make it impractical or impossible to install the facilities required for the operation of a regular darkroom. Specific instructions can be found in the Kodak Professional Data Book G-5, which is available at most photo stores.

Paper developers

Most paper developers are different from film developers, and the two are normally not interchangeable. An exception is the Kodak Versatol developer, which is equally suited for developing films and papers and therefore should be of particular interest to amateurs who want to process both types of material with the least amount of fuss. More discriminating photographers distinguish among paper developers that produce prints in brownish or warm tones, neutral gray or black ones, and bluish or cold tones; these differences, however, are generally slight. Unlike film developers, most of which can be used repeatedly, used paper developers cannot be reused and must be discarded at the end of each printing session. Typical neutral paper developers are Kodak D-72 and Dektol.

Other materials

Acid stop bath. Its purpose is to quickly terminate development by neutralizing the alkaline developer, which has been absorbed by the emulsion and the paper base; to deliver the paper into the fixer in an acid instead of an alkaline condition and thereby prolong the acidity, hardening ability, and useful life of the fixer; and to minimize the possibility of staining in the fixer because of insufficient agitation.

A self-mixed stop bath consists of 30cc of glacial acetic acid (or 125cc of 28% acetic acid) added to one liter of water. Such a bath has a capacity per liter of approximately 20 sheets of 8″ x 10″ paper or its equivalent. Prepared stop baths are made among others by Kodak. One of them—Kodak Indicator stop bath—contains a dye which, by changing with use from yellow to purple-blue, gives warning that the bath is exhausted and ready for replacement by a freshly perpared one.

Fixer or hypo. The purpose of the fixing bath is to convert the undeveloped light-sensitive silver salts of the paper emulsion into water-soluble compounds that can subsequently be removed by washing. Although not too critical, the duration of fixation is important, because, if fixed too briefly, prints will not be permanent; on the other hand, if they are fixed too long, image quality deteriorates through bleaching, the excessively hypo-laden prints require much longer washing times, and the prints are in danger of gradually turning yellow with age.

To assure proper fixation, experienced printmakers use the two-bath system of fixation: In accordance with the instructions that accompany your fixer, prepare two identical fixing baths. Transfer your prints from the acid stop bath to the first fixing bath and leave them there for three to five minutes, agitating them frequently. Then take the papers out of this bath, let them drain until they stop dripping, and transfer them to the second fixing bath where they are left and agitated periodically for another three to five minutes. When the first fixer shows signs of exhaustion (test it from time to time with the aid of one of the commercially available hypo-test solutions), discard it, replace it with the second bath, and prepare a new second bath from fresh hypo.

Hypo-neutralizer (also called hypo-eliminator or hypo-clearing bath). Its purpose is twofold: To insure virtually complete elimination of hypo from the prints, and to shorten the time of the washing process. Specific information for use is always given on the label of the respective product. To produce prints of archival quality *i.e.*, prints whose images will last longer than the paper, Kodak recommends its Hypo Clearing Agent solution followed by treatment in a Hypo Eliminator HE-1 bath.

Ferricyanide. A crystalline, poisonous substance indispensable for the production of high-quality prints, where it is used as a bleach to lighten areas that turned out too dark. Specific instructions for its use are given on p. 104.

Viscose sponges are invaluable aids in any darkroom, where they fulfill two purposes: to soak up accidentally spilled solutions, and to remove surface moisture from prints before they go into the drier or are hung up to dry. Needless to say, different sponges must be used for these purposes, and to avoid the danger of chemical contamination, sponges must be kept scrupulously clean and replaced as soon as they show signs of deterioration.

Absorbent cotton is needed for swabbing developer concentrate on those areas of a developing print that should be darkened to a higher degree than would have been possible with normal development (p. 45); to lighten with ferricyanide print areas that came out too dark (p. 104); and to act as an improvised but quite efficient filter when filtering solutions, for which purpose a tuft of absorbent cotton is placed loosely in the funnel through which the solution that is to be filtered is poured into the storage bottle. For treating small print areas, instead of a wad of cotton, which might be too large, a Q-Tip is very effective.

Tapes of different kinds are invaluable multipurpose aids in a darkroom. I always have three types handy: black photographic or masking tape, inch-wide white surgical tape, and Scotch Magic Transparent Tape No. 810. I use them for everything from making labels for bottles to masking negatives and holding things temporarily in place.

White petroleum jelly (Vaseline), rubbed very lightly on a scratched negative, fills in such marks so that they are either minimized or do not show up at all in the print. A commercially available preparation that serves the same purpose is Scratch-Patch.

Kerodex 71 is the trade name of a protective hand cream that I found extremely effective and pleasant to use. It is available in drugstores.

Dry-mounting tissue is needed for doing a professional job of joining a print to its cardboard mount. Two types are available, one with a rubber-wax base, the other with an inert resin base. I use only the latter, which is more permanent and also protects the print against possible damage resulting from harmful ingredients in the mounting board. In contrast to resin-base dry-mounting tissue, rubber-wax base mounting tissues are impermanent, because the organic rubber is subject to early decomposition. Rubber cement, although temptingly easy to use, will eventually soak through and stain the print. Water-soluble pastes and glues distort the paper and cause print and mount to warp.

Print-spotting colors. I use ordinary watercolors, although special, but disproportionately expensive, print-spotting colors are available in photo stores. Two small tubes of color, black and white, are all that is needed to mix any required shade of gray. For glossy prints, special colors are available that dry glossy.

Pencil and paper are needed constantly: to write data on the back of prints, jot down ideas for future work, make notes about replenishing darkroom supplies. I found the thick, soft lead pencils that editors use particularly suitable. I also like the Committee Bonded Lead Linton 12. Hard pencils are unsuitable, because they easily print through when used on the back of photographic paper; besides, their writing is too thin to be legible in the dim glow of the safelight.

A felt-tipped permanent ink marker, which writes on any surface including metal and glass, is almost indispensable for labelling bottles, cans, cardboard containers, boxes for paper and prints, and so on.

III. How to make a print

Fundamentally, a print is a positive paper replica of a negative. Like a negative, it starts with an exposure, producing a latent image, which subsequently must be developed, fixed, washed, and dried. But unlike a negative, the size of which is determined once and for all by the format of the camera that produced it, a print can be any size, and whereas a negative is unique, any number of prints can be made from the same negative, all originals.

In practice, of course, a print is only more or less a positive replica of the negative from which it was made, since, apart from differences in size, other differences may exist, particularly in regard to sharpness, contrast, density (lightness or darkness), cropping, perspective, and cleanliness. Such differences can either enhance or degrade the technical quality and the artistic effect of a print, depending on whether they are the result of control or incompetence on the part of the photographer. I will have more to say about this later (pp. 70–119).

Although all prints are processed in the same way, for practical reasons we must distinguish between two types:

Contact prints
Projection prints

HOW TO MAKE A CONTACT PRINT

A contact print is identical in size to the negative from which it was made. This fact obviously limits its usefulness, particularly if the negative is small. Consequently, contact prints are used primarily for purposes of reference, in the form of proof prints, or contact sheets, for identifying, classifying, or aiding in filing and retrieving negatives, and for personal use in albums or as wallet-size pictures.

Contact prints are made with the aid of a contact-printer (p. 18) on relatively slow paper (p. 32) and are normally exposed by an ordinary light-bulb. Processing is identical to that of a projection print. Here is a brief summary of the sequence of operations:

Preparations
Turn off the room light, turn on the safelight
Expose the paper
Develop the paper
Transfer the paper to the acid stop bath
Transfer the paper to the fixer
Now you can again turn on the white room light
Transfer the paper to the hypo-neutralizer
Wash the print
Dry the print

More specifically, here is a step-by-step description of making a contact print with the aid of a printing frame:

Preparations by white light

Darken the room (p. 15). Set up five trays for developer, stop bath, fixer, hypo-neutralizer, and water. Prepare the developer (p. 40). Prepare the acid stop bath (p. 40). Prepare the fixer (p. 40). Prepare the hypo-neutralizer (p. 41). Fill the water tray. Check the temperature of the solutions (standard temperature is 68° F.). Clean the negative (p. 52). Examine the negative for contrast in order to be able to select a paper of suitable gradation (p. 94). Select a paper of suitable speed and gradation (pp. 32 and 33).

Place the negative, emulsion (dull) side up in the printing frame, making sure that the glass of the frame is clean and free of dust. If the negative is smaller than the frame size, put the appropriate mask between glass and negative. (If you use a contact printer use its masking strips.) Otherwise, the contact print will have a black edge instead of a white one.

Turn off the white light, turn on the safelight.

Exposing by amber safelight

Open the paper package in such a way that it can be reused for wrapping unused paper, remove one sheet, and place it, emulsion (shiny) side down, on the negative. Handle the paper by the edges only to avoid leaving indelible fingermarks. Close the printing frame. Do not forget to wrap unused paper securely before exposing the print; otherwise, it would be fogged and ruined by the white light.

Place the printing frame, glass side up, beneath the printing lamp, and expose the paper. Duration of the exposure depends on the density of the negative, the speed of the paper, the wattage of the lamp, and the distance between lamp and printing frame. However, since all these factors except for the density of the negative are known and constant, a test will establish once and for all the basic exposure time. For a trial exposure, use a frosted 100 w household bulb four feet from the printing frame and expose for 15 seconds. If you use a contact-printer equipped with a frosted 15 w lamp, try a two-second exposure. To time short exposures, slowly count one-and-twenty, two-and-twenty, and so forth, for one-second intervals, having checked yourself first against the second hand of your watch.

Developing by amber safelight

Take the exposed paper out of the printer, and smoothly slide it edgewise into the developer, emulsion side up. Be careful not to get your hand wet. Use the print tongs (p. 28) to dunk and manipulate the paper. Agitate by gently rocking the tray for the entire duration of the development. Leave the print in the developer for not less than one and not more than two minutes. If by that time the picture is already too dark, the exposure was too long; if it is still too light, the exposure was too short. Wrongly exposed prints cannot be saved; instead, make a new print with a shorter or longer exposure.

Acid stop bath by amber safelight

Using the print tongs, take the print out of the developer, let it drain for a moment, then transfer it to the acid stop bath (p. 40). Make sure that the developer tongs do not come in contact with the stop-bath solution. Hold the print above the stop-bath tray, lower it partly into the solution, then release the print, and let it slide down the rest of the way by itself, immediately dunking it with the fixer tongs. Developer tongs that accidentally touched the acid stop bath must be rinsed briefly before reuse; otherwise, the developer will be spoiled through contamination with stop-bath solution. Using the fixer tongs, agitate the print in the stop bath for 10 to 15 seconds, then transfer it to the fixer (p. 40).

Fixing by amber safelight

Fix the print for five to ten minutes in accordance with the instructions on the fixer package or bottle. Agitate gently for the first minute, then at frequent intervals. If several prints are in the bath, make sure that they do not cling together or lie in a pile at the bottom of the tray. After the last print has been in the fixer for about a minute, you can safely—

Turn on the white light.

Hypo-neutralizer by white light

Transfer the fixed print to the hypo-neutralizer bath (p. 41), and leave it there for 2 to 3 minutes, agitating all the time with the fixer tongs, which should be rinsed briefly before reuse in the fixer.

Washing by white light

Wash single-weight prints for about 10 minutes and double-weight prints for about half an hour under running water of 65° to 75° F. (pp. 35 and 44), using a syphon device (p. 29) to drain the hypo-laden water from the bottom of the tray. To prevent the stream of water from striking the prints, which may crack the emulsion or crease them, place a small jar or other suitable vessel in the tray directly below the faucet to break the force of the stream, letting the water spill over its edges into the tray. Agitate the prints repeatedly and make sure especially that they do not lie in a pile at the bottom of the tray. Careful workers completely drain and refill the tray four or five times during the wash. Alternatively, use the washing tank described in Vol. I. Place the tray or tank in the sink and watch out that prints do not float to the surface, slide over the edge of the tray into the sink, plug the drain, and cause a flood. Air bubbles clinging to the prints should be stroked off with the hands.

Drying by white light

Remove the washed prints from the water, let them drain briefly, then place each print on the bottom of an inverted tray and sponge or squeegee it off from both sides to remove surface water. Place the damp prints in a blotter book or a blotter roll, and leave them to dry overnight.

Above: To find out whether or not the solid black area of a print hides detail which, in a second attempt, might be brought out through "dodging" (p. 97), hold the photograph in front of a lamp and examine it in transmitted light; latent detail will then show clearly.

Right: Determination of the best way of cropping a print is easiest with the aid of two L-shaped cardboard masks. They enable a photographer to isolate and evaluate, by itself, any desired area of a picture.

The contact sheet (gang printing)

Contact sheets are indispensable to any photographer above the level of the occasional snapshooter. They provide him with a record of his work, enable him to compare all the negatives on a roll with one another and decide which ones to enlarge, are an invaluable aid in deciding how to crop a picture, and form the backbone of the negative file, without which nobody would be able to find a specific negative when he needs it.

A contact sheet, or proof sheet, is a multiple contact print of all the negatives on one specific roll, printed together on the same sheet of 8″ x 10″ or 8½″ x 11″ paper. Accordingly, a contact sheet contains either thirty-six 35mm negatives, or twelve 2¼″ x 2¼″ negatives, or four 4″ x 5″ negatives. Normally, a roll of 35mm film is cut into six lengths, each strip containing six negatives; roll film (2¼″ x 2¼″) is cut either into four lengths of three negatives each, or three lengths of four negatives each.

Since it is unlikely that all the negatives on the roll are equal in regard to contrast and density, to minimize such differences, a relatively soft paper (p. 33)—either grade 2 or grade 1—is normally used for making contact sheets. This has the further advantage that it gives a photographer a point of reference for gauging the actual contrast of each negative, making it easier to select an enlarging paper of the most suitable gradation.

To be most practical, orient all the negatives in the same direction. Nothing is more annoying when reading a contact sheet than one or several film strips printed upside-down. Furthermore, the strips should be arranged on the contact sheet in the same sequence in which they originally appeared on the film roll, particularly if the individual negatives are numbered on the film, as is the case with most 35mm films.

Negatives selected for printing can be marked on the contact sheet with a red or black China marking pencil, or grease pencil. If necessary, such marks can later be removed without leaving a trace by wiping either with a piece of tissue paper or, in more stubborn cases, with ordinary household cleaning fluid. The same kind of pencil is, of course, used to indicate specific ways of cropping the future print on the contact sheet.

Opposite page: A typical contact sheet, like the one shown here, is rarely a beautiful sight. Its purpose is to contain as much information as possible in order to enable the photographer to pick the best negatives for enlarging. This will most likely be the case if paper of relatively soft gradation (p. 33) is used that simultaneously holds detail in both highlights and shadows, in underexposed as well as in overexposed negatives. Notice, for example, that in this case there is modulation in the lightest areas of the skin as well as in the originally black leotard. In comparison to this advantage, the often "muddy" appearance of a contact sheet is a small price to pay.

Reading a contact sheet correctly requires experience, not to say talent. Unavoidable differences in contrast and density in conjunction with the smallness of the individual pictures make those frames having the right degree of contrast and density appear better in the contact sheet than they actually are. Photographers who do not make allowance for such accidental excellence often overlook other better and more interesting pictures, for the sole reason that those particular negatives printed too light, too dark, too flat, or too contrasty on the contact sheet. Unless such deviations from the norm are excessive, however, faults of this kind are usually easily corrected during enlarging through appropriate choice of paper gradation and adjustment of print exposure time. Whereas beginners look for the technically most perfect negatives, experienced photographers first scan their contact sheets for pictures that are interesting subjectwise, and mark those negatives for printing, no matter how technically poor they may appear on the contact sheet.

HOW TO MAKE A PROJECTION PRINT (ENLARGEMENT)

A projection print (or enlargement, or blowup) is made with the aid of an enlarger (p. 19) on relatively fast paper (p. 32), and can have any size and proportions. Unlike contact printing, where control is severely restricted, projection printing allows a photographer a considerable amount of control as far as the final appearance of the print is concerned (pp. 78–119). Making the most of this opportunity, especially in regard to contrast, lightness or darkness, and composition (cropping) of the future picture is a sign of an accomplished printmaker. Processing is identical to that of contact prints. Here is a brief summary of the sequence of operations:

Preparations
Turn off the white light, turn on the safelight
Adjust the size of the image
Focus the enlarger lens
Stop down the enlarger lens
Expose the paper
Develop the paper
Transfer the paper to the acid stop bath
Transfer the paper to the fixer
Now you can again turn on the white room light
Transfer the paper to the hypo-neutralizer
Wash the print
Dry the print

As mentioned before, processing of contact prints and projection prints is identical. Therefore, in the following, I can limit myself to discussing those factors unique to projection printing, referring the reader to the foregoing as far as developing, fixing, and so forth are concerned.

Preparations by white light

Follow the instructions given on p. 44. In this respect, the main difference between contact printing and projection printing is in the size of the trays, since enlargements, of course, require larger trays than contact prints. Negatives intended for projection printing must, however, be cleaned much more thoroughly than those intended for contact printing, since the higher the degree of enlargement, the more prominently dirt and dust will appear in the picture.

To clean a negative, brush off loose particles of dust and lint with a camel's-hair brush, working lightly with slow and gentle strokes in order to charge the negative electrically as little as possible, because this would only attract still more dust. This problem is particularly acute on cold and dry days—the more you brush, the more you charge the negative, and the greater its attraction to dust. Under such conditions, use of a special, static-elminating brush with a polonium strip seems to do some good. Also, touching the negative to a grounded conductor (for example, the grounded column of the enlarger) can help to dissipate a static charge. Often, a better method than brushing is to blow dust particles off a negative with the aid of a small rubber syringe, using short, sharp puffs.

The best way to examine a negative for particles of dust and lint is to hold it at a steep angle in the beam of the enlarger lamp just below the lens, sharply sidelighting possible dust particles, which will stand out glaringly white against the blackness of the negative. On very dry days, I find that wiping the negative with an anti-static cloth of the kind used for polishing furniture provides an effective way of preventing the buildup of a static charge. Fresh fingermarks and certain kinds of spots can be removed with a film-cleaner such as Kodak, Ecco 1500 or 1341; old fingermarks that have already eaten into the emulsion are permanent. Abrasion marks and fine scratches can be minimized and, in light cases, even prevented from showing in the print with the aid of Scratch-Patch or by rubbing a fine film of petroleum jelly (Vaseline) on the respective areas of the negative. Afterwards, this greasy film should be removed with cleaning fluid.

Mask the negative. Sparkling prints with pure white highlights and a predetermined contrast range can only be produced if no stray light is permitted to escape from the enlarger. Such stray light would be reflected from the work table, the walls and ceiling of the darkroom, the clothes, hands, and face of the operator, and so on, and would provide a faint but disastrous overall illumination equivalent to an overall exposure of the photographic paper to white light, degrading its highlights and lowering its contrast.

The two most common sources of stray light are the ventilation outlets of the enlarger head, and light passing around or through the negative but outside the area that is to be enlarged. In the first case, the best a photographer normally can do about this problem is to cover the ceiling and upper parts of the darkroom walls with a coat of dull, black paint (instead of white, see Vol. I), unless, of course, he prefers to exchange his badly designed enlarger for a better one. In the second case, he can mask his negative. Glassless negative carriers already mask a negative, provided the entire area of the negative is going to be enlarged. Often, however, a photographer may want to crop his picture in the print, *i.e.*, enlarge only a certain part of the negative. If this is the case, the negative areas that will not appear in the print must be masked, that is, covered by a frame cut out of thin black paper which blocks undesirable enlarger light and prevents it from fogging the print. This kind of mask is, of course, even more important if the negative is held between glass plates, which provide no frame but may let huge amounts of stray light pass around the edges of the film. Excellent sources for masking material are the black inner envelopes or wrappings of enlarging paper and the thin black sheets of paper that separate sheet films from one another in their package. To cut the mask, fold the black paper sharply down the middle, then cut the appropriate opening with a pair of scissors. Unfolded, the paper will form a perfect rectangular frame.

Place the negative in the film carrier, emulsion (dull) side down, facing the lens. In order to have the projected image appear right side up on the easel, turn the negative in the carrier so that the top edge of the picture faces you. (Some negative carriers permit orienting vertical shots only in such a way that the bottom of the image on the easel faces either right or left but cannot face you.) If you put the negative between glass plates (p. 24), make sure they, too, are clean and free from fingermarks and dust. Slowly, in order not to stir up possible dust inside the enlarger, slide the loaded negative carrier into place, and just before you lower the top of the enlarger head, switch on the enlarger lamp, and check the negative once more for dust that might have settled on it since you cleaned it. If everything looks clean, slowly, in order not to stir up dust through a pumping effect, lower the top of the enlarger head onto the negative carrier.

Turn off the white light, turn on the safelight.

Focusing by amber safelight

Making a projection print requires that the enarger be adjusted in two respects: for print size, and for sharpness.

Adjustment for print size. Start by deciding how large you wish to make your print; then adjust the masking strips of the paper easel (p. 27) accordingly. If your easel has adjustable margin stops, set them to the desired margin width. To achieve the necessary degree of enlargement, raise

Sharp—unsharp—blurred. Left: A sharply focused negative reveals the film grain (even though a magnifier may be needed to see it); such a print is called "grain-sharp." *Center:* Unsharpness due to faulty focusing of the enlarger lens; correctly focused, even an unsharp negative would show film grain. *Right:* Print blurred due to inadvertent movement of the enlarger head during exposure shows multiple image.

or lower the enlarger head. Raising increases and lowering decreases the size of the print.

Adjustment for sharpness. Sacrifice a sheet of enlarging paper, and place it backside up on the paper easel. Switch on the enlarger lamp, open the diaphragm of the lens to full aperture for maximum illumination, and focus (raising or lowering) the lens until the projected image appears sharp on the easel. Careful workers do not trust their eyes, but use a focusing magnifier (p. 29), preferably focusing on the film grain. If a negative is excessively dense or does not contain any sharply defined detail, focusing can be very difficult. In such cases, turn off the safelight and focus by enlarger light alone. This will enable your eyes to accommodate better to the dimness of the projected image. If this too is unsatisfactory, focus by substitution, *i.e.,* replace the unsatisfactory negative with a more suitable one; alternatively, use a discarded negative in which you have scratched a few fine lines with a needle point, and focus on the scratches. Having properly adjusted the focus, without disturbing anything, remove the substitute negative and put the right one in its place.

If the negative is placed between glass plates, focusing is normally no

Partial unsharpness due to buckling of the negative in the enlarger; use of a glass-plate negative carrier would have prevented this fault. That the unsharpness of the center area of the picture is not a fault of the negative is apparent from the fact that near and distant parts of the view, like the buildings near the left and right edges of the picture and the church steeple farther away, are both sharp. This would be impossible if the lens of the camera had been focused incorrectly or the diaphragm not stopped down enough.

problem, and properly focused, the print ought to be sharp. But if a glass-less negative carrier is used, the negative might buckle out of the plane of focus and the print, despite the most careful focusing, will be partly or entirely unsharp. Such buckling is caused by heat. This kind of unsharpness can usually be avoided if the negative is given time in the carrier to warm up and adjust itself before it is focused. Once focused, the paper should be exposed promptly, before the negative has time to move again, and the exposure should be as short as possible. Dense negatives, which require long exposures (and therefore are subjected to considerable heat), should only be enlarged between glass plates.

Exposing by amber safelight

Stop down the enlarger lens in accordance with the density of the negative (Vol. I), the speed of the enlarging paper (p. 32), and the degree of image magnification.* Stopping down the lens by two or three stops improves the sharpness of the print for two reasons: Most enlarger lenses perform best at medium apertures, but sharpness deteriorates again if f/stops are very small; and stopping down increases the zone of sharpness in depth, *i.e.*, brings negatives that have buckled from heat back into focus. On the other hand, in order to minimize the potential hazards of negative buckling and fog caused by stray light, exposures should be short. Do not make them too short, though, because, in extreme cases, it would be impossible to dodge or burn in negative areas that require this kind of contrast control (p. 97). Normally, exposure times should be in the neighborhood of 10 seconds (for straight prints) to 25 seconds (for contrast-controlled prints). The most pratcical way to adjust the exposure time accordingly is by means of stopping down the lens: The smaller the f/stop, the longer the exposure, and vice versa.

Make a test strip. Unlike black-and-white film, which has a relatively great exposure latitude, the exposure latitude of photographic papers is extremely small. Practically, this means that the print exposure must be on the nose. Establishing the correct exposure time is the most difficult step in printing. And whereas experienced darkroom technicians are fantastically good at guessing exposure times correctly, beginners, to avoid wasting paper, are advised to make first what is known as a "test strip."

---

* Theoretically, exposure time increases proportionally to the square of the distance between paper and lens; for example, increasing the distance by a factor of three requires increasing the exposure time by a factor of nine. In practice, however, other factors like reciprocity law failure and effective area of the light source make this formula only an approximation.

The test strip

Above left: "Straight" unmanipulated print. *Above right*: Print made on the basis of exposure information derived from a test strip. Notice that the sky and the left foreground are "burned in" (p. 100), the man on horseback and the cattle are "held back" (p. 97).

Below: Four ways of exposing a test strip. Notice that the two strips at the left, which were exposed in increasingly longer steps from top to bottom and bottom to top, respectively, yield no useful information. Only exposures which include the lightest as well as the darkest areas of the negative yield data that have practical value, like the two strips at the right.

A test strip is a piece of photographic paper exposed several times in a series of steps which, when examined by white light, after a two-minute development (standardization of developing time is important!), shows a relatively small area of the negative in different degrees of lightness and darkness. The photographer selects the one he likes best, subsequently using the corresponding exposure time for exposing his print.

To make a test strip, cut a sheet of enlarging paper of suitable gradation into a number of pieces approximately four inches long and two inches wide. On the back of each strip, with a soft lead pencil, write the respective contrast number to avoid disastrous mixups of test strips of different gradations. Place one of these strips on the easel in such a way that it includes both light and dark picture areas, such as highlights and shadows, foreground and background, or earth and sky. Cover the strip with a piece of cardboard, turn on the enlarger light, then lift the cardboard and uncover about one-fifth of the strip, exposing it for 32 seconds. At the end of the 32 seconds, uncover another fifth of the strip and expose for 16 seconds. Repeat this three times more until the entire strip has been exposed in increments of one-fifth, the three remaining parts receiving exposures of eight, four, and four seconds, respectively. Expressed in the form of a graph, this is what you should do:

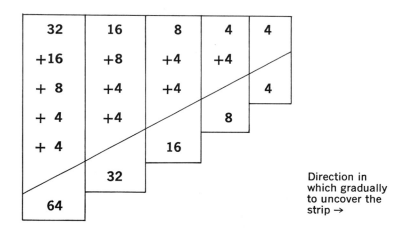

Direction in which gradually to uncover the strip →

Accordingly, the darkest section of your strip received a total of 64 seconds of exposure, the lightest, 4. Intermediate sections received exposures of 32, 16, and 8 seconds, respectively. Develop the test strip, and examine it by white light. With any kind of luck, the correct exposure should be somewhere on this strip; if necessary, interpolate.

58

If you find that the darkest strip of the test print is still too light, repeat the performance but open up the lens by one diaphragm stop. Conversely, if the lightest strip is still too dark, make another test with the lens aperture decreased by one stop. Incidentally, this test strip should also be evaluated in terms of contrast: If it appears generally too gray, the paper grade is too soft for the particular negative; if it appears too contrasty, grade is too hard. In such cases, expose another test strip on paper of a more suitable grade.

As an aid to memory, many photographers make it a habit to write data like paper make and gradation, degree of enlargement, f/stop number, and exposure times on the back of the test strip prior to development, using a soft lead pencil and writing lightly in order not to print through. Then they process the strip and file it together with the respective negative for future use and reference.

An alternate method of determining the correct print exposure involves the use of a Kodak Projection Print Scale, a piece of film divided into ten pie-shaped sectors of different densities through which the test strip (which in this case should be square) is exposed for exactly one minute. The number of the sector which, after development of the test strip, appears best is the required exposure time in seconds.

Still another method of determining the correct print exposure time is based on the use of a special enlarging meter. However, the complexity of all the factors involved in the computation of the final reading—the nature of the subject, the contrast range of the negative, the particular distribution of dense and thin negative areas, the fact that there hardly is a negative that cannot profit from local contrast control (dodging and burning-in, p. 97) and, especially, the personal preferences and opinions of the photographer himself—make determination of print exposure by on-easel photometry a hazardous undertaking.

Place the enlarging paper on the easel, and make the exposure in accordance with the time determined with the aid of the test strip. Stand motionless while you count off seconds or watch the timer, and touch neither the enlarger nor the bench or table on which it stands: Even the slightest vibration is sufficient to cause a slight degree of blur in the print, which would then no longer be grain-sharp. The best way of exposing is by means of a foot switch. Lacking such a device, hold a piece of cardboard directly below the lens, turn on the enlarger lamp, get set to time the exposure, then admit light to the paper by withdrawing the cardboard, being careful not to bring it in contact with the lens. Terminate the exposure by reversing this sequence.

To cover the exposed paper with developer evenly and rapidly, tilt the tray slightly to the left, place the edge of the paper against the left side of the tray, then quickly lower both tray and paper, letting the developer flow smoothly across the future print.

Developing by amber safelight

Follow the instructions given on p. 45. Large paper sizes are, of course, more difficult to handle than small ones. Specifically, care must be taken to insure that the paper is covered by the developer as quickly, smoothly, and evenly as possible. If the volume of solution in the tray is too small, dry islands may persist for a while before the paper is evenly covered, which subsequently may appear as lighter areas in the print, particularly if the paper was not fully developed because it turned rapidly too dark and the photographer tried to save the print by pulling it prematurely.

Acid stop bath by amber safelight

Follow the instructions given on p. 45. User-mixed acid stop baths should be prepared immediately before each printing session (Vol. I) and discarded afterwards. A Kodak Indicator Stop Bath can be used until it changes from yellow to purple-blue, a sign that it is exhausted. Use of an overly strong bath, as well as lack of agitation, may cause water-soak, a condition showing as a mottle on the back of the print, which in time may turn into a yellow stain.

Fixing by amber safelight

Follow the instructions given on p. 46. Place the print face down in the fixer, and dunk it with the fixer tongs. Prints that are left face up tend to float and partly rise above the surface, leaving areas uncovered which might get only incompletely fixed and would later turn yellow. For enlargements that should be permanent, use the two-bath system of fixing described on p. 40. On the other hand, as pointed out before, do not leave prints unnecessarily long in the fixer, since this might cause gradual loss of detail in the light areas of the print and also lead to water-soak. Furthermore, exceeding the recommended fixing time also prolongs the washing time of the prints. After the print has been in the hypo for at least one minute, you may safely—

Turn on the white light.

Hypo-neutralizer by white light

Follow the instructions given on p. 46. An excellent hypo-neutralizer is Kodak Hypo Clearing Agent; according to the manufacturer, prints treated in this solution prior to washing attain a degree of freedom from residual chemicals almost impossible to achieve by washing them in water alone. Do not forget that washing time can also be cut drastically, and colder water be used without any ill effects. Other hypo-neutralizers are Heico Perma-Wash and FR's Hypo Neutralizer.

Washing by white light

Follow the instructions given on p. 46. The longest wash and the most rapid flow of water are meaningless if prints are permitted to cling together or lie in a pile at the bottom of the washer. Whereas the stream of running water may adequately agitate and separate prints up to 5″ x 7″ large, larger prints need frequent handling to insure adequate washing. Overloading the washer with prints prevents proper washing and is a common cause of yellow stain. Adding fresh prints from the fixer to prints that have already been in the washer for some time requires starting the entire washing cycle anew because of water contamination with hypo.

Drying by white light

Follow the instructions given on p. 46. Blotter rolls large enough to take prints up to 16″ x 20″ are available. If time is of the essence, an electric print drier will speed up the drying process considerably. The only truly satisfactory electric driers are large professional drum driers. Small drum driers of the kind usually sold to amateurs are, in my opinion, unacceptable. Flatbed driers differ enormously in quality, but even the best ones are not very good, failing particularly insofar as prints often dry with a wavy edge. This can be avoided if the prints are taken out of the drier while they are still damp, placed between lintless blotters, and left there under pressure until dry. The canvas aprons or belts of all types of electric driers are a potential source of hypo contamination if inadequately washed prints are dried; carefully washed prints may pick up traces of fixer from the hypo-impregnated canvas apron or belt and in time develop a yellow stain, much to the surprise of the photographer who thought he had done everything to make them permanent. A space-consuming but otherwise excellent method of drying prints is to hang small prints by one and larger prints by two corners with wooden clips from wires. Drying should proceed slowly since rapid drying in hot air promotes buckling and waviness. When the prints are completely dry, dampen their backs with a moist viscose sponge, being careful to keep the emulsion side dry, and place the prints between blotters. Weight the stack down with a few large books, and leave them until dry.

To a greater or lesser degree, all prints have a tendency to curl. This tendency can be lessened if two prints are dried back to back hanging from the same clip or clips, although drying time will, of course, be prolonged. Prints that have developed a strong curl can be straightened as follows: First, to avoid cracking the emulsion, briefly pass the print, emulsion side down, through the steam rising from a pot of hot but not yet boiling water, making sure that the pass is quick enough not to dampen the print excessively or to deposit droplets of water on the emulsion. Then place the print, emulsion side up, flat on a table that has a straight and fairly sharp edge free of nicks and splinters, and pull it by one corner diagonally across the edge at a downward angle of approximately 60 degrees, placing your left hand flat on the print and pushing and guiding it slowly across the edge while your right hand pulls. When drying prints in an electric flatbed drier, take the prints out and straighten them before they are completely dry. If you missed the right moment, place the bone-dry prints, emulsion side down, for a moment on the canvas apron of the drier immediately after it has been freshly loaded with wet prints; steam rising from the apron will almost instantly moisten the dry prints sufficiently to prevent cracking the emulsion during the straightening process.

Ferrotyping prints. This process, which requires the use of ferrotype plates, gives prints on glossy paper a mirror-like finish. (Other surfaces cannot be ferrotyped.) In essence, it consists of pressing the wet prints tightly against a polished surface and leaving them there until dry when they will come off by themselves. The main problem is to avoid matte spots in the glossy finish of the prints caused by air trapped between paper and ferrotype plate. To avoid such marks, proceed as follows:

Make sure that the ferrotype plate (or the chromium-plated drum of a drum-type drier) is perfectly clean—free of residue carried over from the wash water and particles of gelatin deposited there by previously treated prints, which would cause the fresh prints to stick to the plate. Once stuck, the only way to get a print off the plate or drum is to soak the paper with water and rub it off piece by piece. Trying to scrape it off with a sharp instrument would scratch the ferrotyping surface and ruin it forever. A good ferrotype plate cleaner is Glass Wax, a liquid normally used for window cleaning and available anywhere.

Heat up the print-drier to a plate or drum temperature not exceeding 180° F. Place the ferrotype plate on a flat surface that cannot be damaged by water (I use the large sheet of Lucite that covers my fixer and hypo-neutralizer trays when they are not in use; see Vol. I). Scoop up some water from the washer, and sprinkle it over the ferrotype plate. Take one print at a time from the washer and transfer it as rapidly as possible to the ferrotype plate in order to carry to the plate a good amount of water. Hold the print vertically by two adjacent corners, touch it to the ferrotype plate near one edge, then lower it gradually, and roll it onto the plate. The idea is to preserve as large as possible a layer of water immediately in front of the zone of contact between paper and plate, using it to drive possible air bells in front of it and thereby preventing air from getting trapped between the ferrotype plate and the print. When the print is down flat, squeeze it to the plate with a print roller; if the print is large, start at the center and roll toward the edges in order to squeeze out possible pockets of air. If several small prints are going to be ferrotyped together on the same plate, first remove surface water by blotting with a viscose sponge, then cover the prints with a sheet of blotting paper before rolling them into place to prevent them from adhering to the roller and coming off the plate. Subsequently, place the ferrotype plate in the drier and leave it there until the prints are dry when they will pop off by themselves.

Unsatisfactory results of ferrotyping are usually due to one of three mistakes. (1) The drier has overheated, causing the print to come off the ferrotype plate in steps; these steps leave irregular, more or less concentric cracks in the glossy surface of the print. Since they resemble the growth layers of an oyster shell, they are called "oystershell marks." (2) The processing solutions are overworked. An exhausted stop bath is no longer able to remove scum from the paper surface, which, carried all along the line, ultimately causes matte spots in the ferrotyped print. And an exhausted fixing bath cannot harden the print emulsion sufficiently, with the result that the print may stick to the hot ferrotype plate, or leave traces of gelatin on the plate which may cause subsequently dried prints to stick. (3) Air trapped between print and ferrotype plate, usually because of working too dry or insufficient rolling, causes matte spots and streaks in the glossy surface. Immersing the prints briefly in a wetting-agent solution between washing and drying will aid considerably in preventing this fault. And prints washed in only slowly running water or left lying in stagnant water for any length of time may pick up large quantities of air bells; such accumulations of air should be wiped off with the flat of the hand and the prints briefly reimmersed before they are transferred to the ferrotype plate.

Spotting

A print that comes off the drier spotlessly clean is a rarity, no matter how careful the photographer. Most prints have at least a few minor light or dark spots, caused either by dust particles adhering to the film in the camera, which will appear as dark spots in the print, or to the negative in the enlarger, which will appear as light spots in the print. Such blemishes should be removed by spotting.

Dark spots are eliminated with the aid of an etching knife or a single-edge razorblade. Gently scrape the surface of the print with the point of the knife or a corner of the razorblade (which can be kept sharp by breaking off worn corners), until the dark spot has been lightened sufficiently to blend with its surroundings. Care must be taken to work very lightly and not to dig through the emulsion down to the paper base. Practice first on inferior prints, until you have learned to shave off almost invisibly thin layers of emulsion. Do not try to scrape the spot off with a single stroke; it cannot be done. Should you overdo the shaving and the spot is suddenly too light, darken it with a No. 4 lead pencil or a touch of watercolor in the appropriate shade of gray. If the corrections show up objectionably matte on a shiny surface, they can be made invisible by spraying the print with an appropriate lacquer. Suitable print lacquer in spray cans is available in most photo stores.

Light spots are eliminated with the aid of watercolor or, in the case of glossy prints, spotting dye, applied with a high-quality No. 1 size sable brush. Special, more expensive spotting colors are available in photo stores. Match the tone of the surrounding surface by mixing appropriate amounts of black and white, keeping in mind that most colors darken somewhat as they dry. Try to work as dry as possible, taking up only minute amounts of pigment with the point of the brush, twirling it to shape the tip into a fine point. Touch the spot lightly, and apply color in a very thin layer in the form of minute, tightly spaced dots rather than strokes; if necessary, feather the color until the spot blends with the surrounding area. If, after drying, the correction is too light, darken it with a No. 4 pencil or a dash of darker watercolor; if it is too dark, gently shave it with a razorblade before you apply another, lighter coat in order to avoid raising an ugly lump of paint on the print.

Trimming and mounting

To trim prints, use a paper trimmer (cutting board) or a single-edge razorblade in conjunction with a steel straightedge, with the print placed on a smooth, hard surface. Glass is best, but the razorblade will get dulled pretty fast. It can be sharpened simply by breaking off the worn corner. Trimming is often required, for several reasons: (1) You may have to equalize the width of a white border all around the print; white-bordered prints are usually preferred for albums, portraits, and amateur photo exhibitions. (2) You may want to trim the white border off the print; borderless prints are usually preferred for commercial purposes, presentation portfolios, and the more sophisticated type of photo exhibition. (3) You may need to rejuvenate a print (with or without a white border) whose edges have become worn from frequent handling; trimming off a narrow strip all around will often make the print appear like new.

If you wish to mount your prints, start by selecting the board. For flush-mounted, *i.e.*, borderless, prints, almost any kind of cardboard will do, the main consideration being thickness. If the mount shows in the form of a border, consider the tone, color, and texture of the mounting board. In these respects, keep in mind that a white border, by contrast with its own brightness, makes a print appear darker. Its lightest areas, unless they are pure white, may appear gray and even muddy. Conversely, mounted on black, a print appears generally lighter and its lightest areas almost luminous. A board in a medium gray shade presents both the lightest and the

Common mistakes in printing.

Top left: Too little developer in tray, paper not evenly covered; result: a streaky print.

Above: Dust and lint settled on the negative in the enlarger; result: a spotty print.

Left: Sensitized paper touched with wet hands; result: fingermarks on the print.

Opposite page, left: Paper underexposed; result: print too light and, if "forced" in the developer, yellow-stained.

Opposite page, right: Paper overexposed, then "pulled" prematurely from the developer; result: a contrastless, mottled and often brownish, discolored print.

darkest areas of the print to good advantage. Colored mounts (including ivory) easily appear arty and should normally be avoided. Smooth boards are much more sensitive to pressure damage, smudges, and fingermarks than rough or pebbled mounts. In my opinion, high-contrast prints usually appear most effective on white or black; medium-contrast prints on either white, gray, or black if their highlights are pure white, and on gray or black if they are not; low-contrast prints appear to best advantage on black. To find the most suitable mount, place the print successively on boards of different shades, and pick the combination you like best.

Prints can be mounted in several ways, of which dry-mounting is most convenient for sizes up to 16″ x 20″. Prints larger than 16″ x 20″ are better wet mounted with Kodak Rapid Mounting Cement, ordinary wallpaper paste, or printer's padding compound. Rubber cement and ordinary household cements and glues are unsuitable for photographic purposes, because they are chemically active and would in time destroy the print.

To dry-mount a print, place it face down on a smooth, hard surface, and cover its back with a sheet of dry-mounting tissue. With the aid of a hot tacking iron or the tip of an ordinary household iron, tack the tissue to the print in two diagonally opposed spots. Turn the print face up, and trim print and tissue together to the correct size and proportions. Place this sandwich in its proper position on the mounting board (see below), hold it in place, lift the corner of the print opposite one of the corners you tacked to the tissue, and tack that corner of the dry-mounting tissue to the board; repeat with the diagonally opposite corner. Place print and mount face up in the dry-mounting press, cover the print with a double thickness of heavy Kraft wrapping paper (which must be free of wrinkles or creases), and close the press. Bonding takes approximately one minute at a press temperature of 200° to 275° F. for black-and-white prints, half a minute at 200° F. for color prints. Alternatively, place mount and print face up on a smooth, hard surface, cover it with a double thickness of Kraft wrapping paper, and weld print and mount together with a household iron set between "Silk" and "Wool" for black-and-white prints and at "Synthetic fabrics" for color prints, working from the center of the print outward.

The proper positioning of a print on the mounting board is, of course, a matter of personal taste. Normally, however, the picture will appear to best advantage if it is centered laterally, if the border is slightly narrower at the top than at the sides, and if it is widest at the bottom.

THE PERMANENCE OF PRINTS

Like negative permanence, print permanence starts with correct processing. To recapitulate briefly: Expose the print in such a way that development is completed in not less than one and not more than two minutes. Use an acid stop bath (p. 40). Fix in accordance with the two-bath system described on p. 40, agitating properly and making sure that the prints are completely submerged and do not stick together at any time. However, equally important as sufficient fixing is avoiding overfixing, which degrades image quality, leads to water-soak (p. 156) often followed by yellow stain, and prolongs washing time. After a brief rinse, treat the fixed prints first in Kodak Hypo Clearing Agent solution followed by a brief wash and then in Kodak Hypo Eliminator HE-1. Wash thoroughly under running water at a temperature of 68° to 72° F. for at least half an hour, handling the prints frequently and making sure that they do not cling together at any time. To make the prints less vulnerable to attack by corrosive atmospheric gases, follow up with a bath in Kodak Gold Protective Solution GP-1 in accordance with the accompanying instructions.

Prints to be processed for archival quality should never be dried in an electric drier, unless the drier is used for nothing else. Hypo absorbed by the canvas apron or belt from less carefully treated prints would contaminate the clean prints and nullify all the previous work. Instead, hang them by clips from overhead wires, and leave them to dry slowly overnight, in quiet air that is neither too warm nor too dry. This has the further advantage that the dry prints may have a curl but will not be wavy-edged as prints that have been dried electrically are apt to be. Straightening a curl is no problem: Lightly dampen the back of each print with a viscose sponge, place the prints between photographic blotters weighted down with some books, and leave them until dry. Stay away from commercial print-flattening solutions, which contain chemicals that can be harmful to prints.

Since a mount protects a print against many types of accidental damage like tearing, dog-earing, edge damage, attack by gaseous chemicals from the back, and fingermarks, it is advisable to mount archival-quality prints on boards. However, care must be taken to use the right kind of board and bonding, since the wrong kinds (and there are many) contain chemicals detrimental to the permanence of the prints. I use nothing but Kodak Dry Mounting Tissue in conjunction with a high-quality Bristol board or—and this may come as a surprise—a sheet of photographic paper of the same kind as that used to make the print. This paper must be processed for archival quality just like the print it will support except, of course, that it does not have to be exposed or treated in a Kodak Gold Protective solution bath. The advantage of such a sandwich consisting of two sheets of photographic paper pasted back to back by dry-mounting tissue is that it stays flat permanently and under all conditions; where even prints mounted on double-thick Bristol boards will curl, back-to-back-mounted photographic paper stays flat, because the forces of humidity that act on the emulsion manifest themselves equally front and back and thereby neutralize one another, since the two surfaces they attack are hygroscopically identical.

Finally, to shield archival-quality prints from dust, fingerprints, and abrasion marks, they should each be protected by a sheet or envelope of clear acetate (available in any artists material supply store) and kept in a dry, cool, and dark place. Displayed on a wall and subject to prolonged exposure to light, even the most carefully prepared print will fade.

IV. Creative print control

All the aspects of printmaking discussed so far have been of a technical nature. By following the respective instructions, a photographer should be in a position to produce prints that are snappy, clean, and unassailable from a phototechnical point of view. But does this mean that his prints will also express his intentions, conveying to the viewer what he saw in the depicted subject and felt in its presence? Not necessarily. For the simple reasons that a snappy picture cannot reflect every kind of mood; that no standards exist for the overall lightness or darkness of a print; that contrast must be in accordance with the nature of the depicted subject; that a black-and-white print can never be more than an interpretation of reality; and that people are different and may interpret reality differently.

In photography, technique is a tool of creativity. Having mastered the technical side of his craft, the next question the student photographer must ask himself should therefore be: How can I apply my newly gained knowledge to best advantage? In other words, *before* he selects the paper with the most suitable gradation or decides the exposure time of his print, a photographer must know how contrasty (or contrastless) and how light (or how dark) he wants his print to be, and must consequently be able to evaluate his freshly made print in these respects in order to ascertain whether he achieved his goal or has to try again.

INSPECTION AND EVALUATION OF PRINTS

The moment to decide whether or not a print is satisfactory is when it has been in the fixer for about one minute. At this time the photographer can switch on the white light, with the data connected with the making of this particular print still fresh in his mind. The negative is still in the enlarger, and producing a new and better print is relatively easy, because it requires nothing more than small variations in an already established procedure. I evaluate a freshly made print as follows:

70

Print inspection. Wet enlargements just out of the fixer are slapped on a sheet of Lucite and compared with one another by white light. The well-shielded lamp is operated by means of a foot switch.

In my own darkroom, I slap the wet print on a 20″ x 30″, quarter-inch thick Lucite sheet. Normally, this sheet covers the fixer and hypo-neutralizer trays when they are not in use, but during a printing session it leans in nearly vertical position against the wall behind these trays. (Another practical arrangement is to slap the wet print onto the back of a large processing tray leaning against the back wall of the sink.) Above this display panel, mounted to the shelf that runs the entire length of the sink, is a well-shielded white light connected to a foot switch which illuminates the print without reflecting glare into my eyes.

My first question is usually: Was the exposure correct? The answer is yes, if the paper was developed not less than one and not more than two minutes, and the overall appearance of the picture is neither too light nor too dark. If, after a two-minute development, the picture is still too light, the exposure was too short; conversely, if, after a one-minute development, the picture is already too dark, the exposure was too long. Attempts to save an under-exposed print through prolonged development (called "forcing") are futile and would only yield a chalky and possibly yellow-stained picture; similarly, trying to save an overexposed print by taking it out of the developer prematurely would only yield a flat and grayish, often mottled and always dirty-looking print. In other words, a wrongly-exposed print should not even make it into the fixer but should go from the developer straight into the waste can.

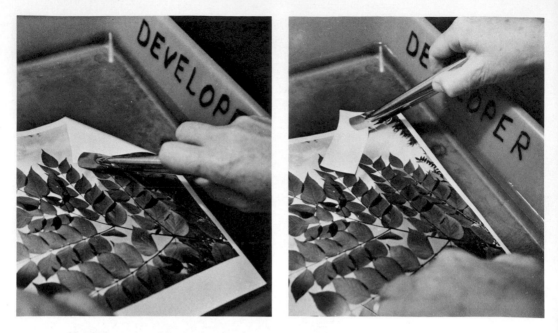

Check for pure white in the developer. Left: Comparison of the lightest area of the print with the carefully bent-over, white underside of the paper. *Right*: Comparison by means of a piece of unexposed, processed, and washed, white photographic paper held against the suspected, white area of the developing print.

My next consideration is contrast. If the subject contained areas or highlights of pure white, I want these to be pure white in my print, too. Unfortunately, the eye is easily deceived about the degree of whiteness in a print and will accept surprisingly dark shades of gray as white, unless it has something really white to compare them with. One such pure white scale of reference is the back side of the paper. Turn over one corner of the print, carefully, so as not to damage the emulsion, and hold the back side of the paper next to the highlight area in the print. This provides an easy gauge of the actual shade of the area in question.

Another method is to run an *unexposed* test strip (pp. 56, 58) together with the first print of the day through the fixer, and use this pure white piece of photographic paper as a gauge; it can be left in the fixer until the last print has been made and subsequently either washed, dried, and used again the next time, or discarded.

Next, disregarding pure whites and blacks, I examine the light and dark areas of the print in regard to detail. Is there sufficient differentiation within the brightly illuminated subject areas as well as in the shadows? If the light areas are deficient in this respect, nothing can be done about it except remake the print, giving the respective areas additional exposure through burning in (p. 100). If the shadows are lacking in detail, however, appropriate treatment with a ferrocyanide solution (p. 104) can sometimes save the print.

When considering the density (overall lightness or darkness) of his prints—whether during development or subsequent examination—a photographer must take into account that, under safelight illumination, a print always appears somewhat darker than in white light. In other words, a print that seemed just right in the developer will probably appear too light when dry and viewed in daylight, whereas a print that appeared somewhat on the dark side in the developer will probably be just right. This phenomenon has nothing to do with the color of the safelight but is due to the fact that everything appears darker in dim light than in bright light.

A different kind of surprise may be in store for the photographer who, for one reason or another, insists on printing his negatives on semi-matte or matte paper. Due to the nature of their surface, such papers have a softer gradation than glossy papers and, when dry, appear less contrasty. Their darkest areas are never more than a dark shade of gray, and even their highlights seem less bright than those of glossy paper. Unfortunately, as long as they are wet, prints made on semi-matte and matte paper appear just as snappy as dry prints on glossy paper, giving a totally erroneous impression of what the ultimate effect will be.

I always judge the overall lightness or darkness of a print on the basis of the specific mood I am after. If I want to achieve a documentary or matter-of-fact impression, I try for a somewhat lighter print than when I am striving for a more mysterious or dramatic effect. This is the moment when instinctive feeling and creativeness are more important than book knowledge and rationalization—when individuality is king and disagreement among photographers high. A print that one viewer likes because of its joyful lightness may be rejected as underexposed by another, and a print that seems too dark to one photographer may seem too light to another.

As a matter of fact, drawing the right conclusion when examining prints fresh out of the fixer can be so difficult that even experienced photographers often "buy insurance" by making several, slightly different prints—some lighter, some darker, some a little bit more burned in here or held back there (p. 97), or perhaps another print made on paper of softer or harder gradation. They examine these prints side by side on the display panel, compare them with one another, then possibly decide to make still more prints with additional corrections, until they arrive at the perfect print.

73

Lighter or darker print? Whereas normally the acceptable span between the overall lightness and darkness of a picture is rather small, subjects exist which can tolerate much greater variations and still yield significant prints. Of the two versions of the New York skyline at night shown here, for example, the lighter one makes a positively radiant impression, whereas the darker one, although perfectly acceptable, is more conventional and rather dull.

THE NINE POSITIVES

The foregoing should make it abundantly clear that the graphic effect of any print is the combined result of several factors:

Contrast of the negative
Gradation of the paper
Exposure time of the print
Time of the development (to some extent)

Each of these factors is influenced by and in turn influences all the others. By making use of the characteristics of these factors and combining them in predetermined ways, creative photographers can achieve virtually any imaginable graphic effect, from harshest black and white to softest gray on gray, from high-key to low-key, from the richest tonal gradation to monotony.

It is very easy to ascertain whether a correctly developed print made from a negative of normal contrast on paper of normal gradation is correctly, over- or underexposed. It is considerably more difficult to determine whether a print that appears contrastless and too light is underexposed, underdeveloped, printed on paper of unsuitable gradation, or whether the unfortunate effect is perhaps the result of a combination of several of these mistakes. And although it seems hard to believe, it is a fact that underexposure and overexposure can occur simultaneously in one and the same print. This happens every time a contrasty negative is printed on paper of hard gradation. In such a case, the dark subject areas (because they are too dark) will appear in the print as if they were overexposed and the light subject areas (because they are too light) will appear as if they were underexposed.

To give the reader an idea of how the different combinations of print exposure and paper gradation look in the form of actual photographs, I will show what is known as "the nine positives"—the nine basic combinations of correct, over-, and underexposure in conjunction with paper of normal, soft, and hard gradation. This, of course, leaves out one important factor: negative contrast. To visualize the full spectrum of all the possible graphic effects, the reader must imagine a second demonstration like this but based upon the use of a negative of higher than normal contrast, and a third one involving a negative of lower than normal contrast. Not to mention the possibility of smaller or larger differences in print exposure and/or negative contrast, and these again in combination with paper of five different gradations instead of only three . . .

Low contrast (soft) ◄—**Paper gradation**—► Normal **High contrast (hard)**

Too short (underexposure)

◄—**Print exposure**—► Correct

Too long (overexposure)

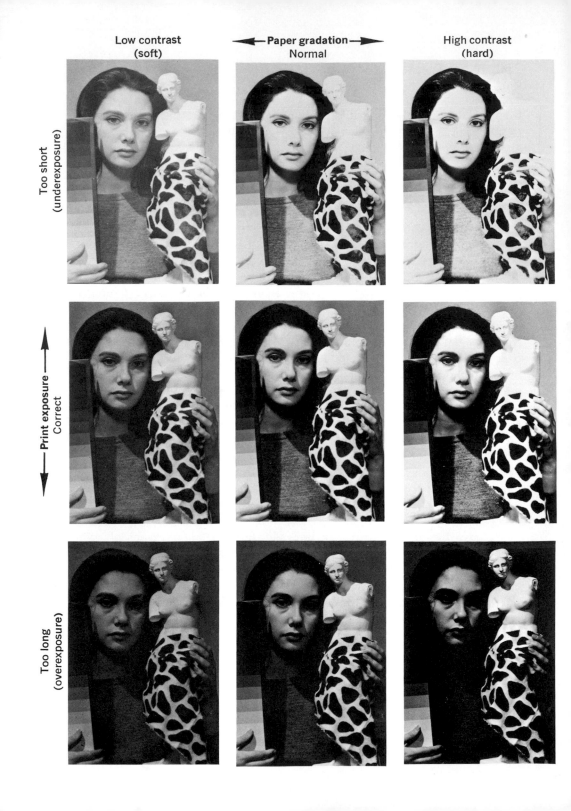

The nine positives

From left to right and top to bottom, these are the nine possible combinations of paper gradation and print exposure and their results in terms of contrast and lightness or darkness of the picture. In addition to the examples shown here, any number of intermediate, as well as more extreme, stages are, of course, possible.

1. Paper too soft, print underexposed. The general impression is one of extreme weakness. Tones are "muddy" and black and white never occur together in the same print.

2. Paper gradation normal, print underexposed. General impression: the print appears too light, gray shades are inadequately represented.

3. Paper too hard, print underexposed. General impression: extremely harsh and contrasty, the image consists of virtually pure black and white.

4. Paper too soft, print correctly exposed. General impression: too dark, too "muddy," and too weak.

5. Paper gradation normal, print correctly exposed. General impression: the print is satisfactory in regard to contrast and tonal differentiation.

6. Paper too hard, print correctly exposed. General impression: a little bit too snappy, tonal differentiation inadequate within the lightest and darkest shades.

7. Paper too soft, print overexposed. General impression: much too dark, too "muddy," and too soft.

8. Paper gradation normal, print overexposed. General impression: a little bit dark, perhaps, but "rich" in regard to tonal shades and not exactly unpleasant.

9. Paper too hard, print overexposed. General impression: too dark and too contrasty, gray shades inadequately represented.

The problem of print size. How large should—or can—an enlargement be? Whereas the "should" depends on the purpose of the picture and the nature of the subject, the "can" depends primarily on the degree of sharpness and graininess of the negative. How far a photographer can go in this respect is demonstrated by the three pictures on this spread: the left one shows the photograph in its entirety, the one in the middle a sectional enlargement of the same negative, and the one on the opposite page an even smaller section still more strongly magnified. Whether or not the resulting degree of sharpness and graininess is acceptable depends, of course, on the photographer or his client.

THE PRACTICE OF CREATIVE PRINT CONTROL

I mentioned a moment ago that experienced photographers often make several enlargements from the same negative, all slightly different, in order to make sure that they get the best possible print. In other words, *they experiment.* And the student photographer can do no better than follow their example. This chapter introduces him to the sometimes spectacular effects that a knowledgeable phototechnician can coax out of seemingly ordinary negatives.

To be able to get the fullest benefit from the possibilities open to him through the following techniques, a photographer must perform his own experiments—exercises in print control—*not* with the aim of immediately producing finished prints, but to learn, to compare, to find out what can and cannot be done, how far he can go in each instance before he reaches a limit, and what the ultimate result will be. Once he knows how to produce a certain effect, sooner or later his chance to use it profitably will come. Consequently, the reader is urged to pick a suitable negative—a negative of average contrast depicting an interesting subject of strong and simple forms—and go to work.

Print size. Enlarging makes a photographer independent of camera size. In the good old days, whenever a large print was required, a camera taking the same film size had to be used, since enlarging was an unknown art. Today, any competently made 35mm negative can be blown up to photomural size. What are the consequences of this exhilarating freedom?

The size of an enlargement is determined by two factors: purpose and the state of the negative. Snapshots usually are enlarged only to wallet or photo-album size (the so-called "jumbo" prints). For purposes of reproduction in newspapers, magazines, and books, the standard size is 8″ x 10″ or, rarely, 11″ x 14″. For commercial purposes, advertising, displays, exhibitions, wall decoration, and so forth, the sky is the limit.

Enlarging brings out the best and the worst in a negative. In contact-print size, even a potentially fabulous photograph is bound to be ineffective. Conversely, blown up to the size of a wall, even the picture of an ordinary landscape can look impressive. Experience has shown that, normally, any picture gains by being enlarged up to the natural size of the subject it represents; blown up beyond this size (and this is particularly true in portraiture), it easily appears pretentious or grotesque. However, there are exceptions. Small objects of nature whose scale is neither known to the viewer of the picture nor indicated indirectly in the print (for example, by the size of the fingers holding the object), can appear absolutely spectacular in photographic form when enlarged several or many times their natural size. On the other hand, enlarging small man-made objects to comparable degrees of magnification is usually ineffective, because it glaringly exposes the crudity of such objects, particularly if we compare them with the miniature marvels of nature, which unendingly reveal additional and finer detail, the more they are enlarged.

That a negative which should be greatly enlarged must be technically perfect goes without saying. This applies particularly in regard to two qualities: sharpness and graininess. The first deteriorates and the second becomes more evident directly proportional to the degree of magnification. However, since large prints and particularly photomurals are normally viewed from greater distances than ordinary prints, loss in image quality due to high degrees of magnification is usually offset by the fact that the ability of the eye to resolve fine detail decreases proportionally to increases in the viewing distance. Add to this the fact that the lenses of all good 35mm cameras are considerably sharper than those computed for larger formats, and that the grain pattern of a high-resolution 35mm film is considerably tighter than that of an ordinary 4″ x 5″ negative, and it should not come as a surprise to hear that large prints and photomurals, viewed from the appropriate distance, can appear sharp regardless of the size of the negative. Convincing proof of this are the movies: examined at the normal reading and viewing distance of eight inches, the image is unbelievably crude; but seen projected, from a seat in the theater, it appears perfectly sharp. Worry about sharpness and graininess should therefore not detain anybody from making and enjoying large prints.

Print proportions. Enlarging makes a photographer independent not only of the *size* of his camera and film, but also of the *proportions* of his negatives and photographic paper. Most film formats have one of three proportions: 1:1½ (35mm negatives), 1:1¼ (4″ x 5″ and 8″ x 10″ negatives), and 1:1 (2¼″ x 2¼″ negatives), while the proportions of the standard paper sizes of 8″ x 10″ and 11″ x 14″ are either exactly or very nearly 1:1¼. In the long run, seeing all one's pictures in these stereotyped proportions can become pretty dull.

The first to discover this freedom from dependence on the format of their cameras are usually those photographers working with 2¼″ x 2¼″ film who have been told that the square is dull because it lacks tension. This is, of course, a half-truth since squares do not have to be tensionless. Obviously, a square view of an ordinary landscape with the horizon dividing the picture into equal parts is dull. Sometimes this is precisely the impression the photographer wants to create, dullness having been the outstanding quality of that respective landscape. But a suitable subject squarely and centrally composed can have all the tension of a rifle target where the bull's-eye almost hypnotically draws attention to the center of a square piece of paper—an effect that is anything but dull. In other cases, of course, the square may be unsuited to expressing the essence of the depicted subject or event, and enlarging only a section of a square negative to the proportions of a more elongated rectangle becomes the obvious solution to the problem. Conversely, it can also be advantageous to make a rectangular negative yield a square print by means of suitable cropping.

Print size can be an important factor in determining the effect of a picture. This is particularly true of landscape photographs: if printed too small, the effect of even the most beautiful landscape is severely diminished, if not lost; conversely, enlarged to photo-mural size, even an undistinguished landscape appears impressive.

Rectangles come in an unlimited number of different proportions ranging from square to extremely long and narrow; each format, of course, can be used either in the form of a horizontal or a vertical picture. The narrower and proportionally longer or higher the photograph, the more pronounced the feeling of width or height, an effect that lends itself to many creative applications. For example, cropping strips off the top and bottom of an ordinary rectangular view can make a shot actually made with a lens of standard focal length appear as if it had been made with an extreme wide-angle lens, by drawing attention to the lateral expanse of the scene.

Experienced photographers find the most effective proportions for their pictures by trial and error, working either with contact prints or special work prints—5″ x 7″ or 8″ x 10″ enlargements quickly made without much regard for the finer points of printmaking. They use strips of paper (or the pair of L-shaped cardboard masks described below) to mask off varying areas of each photograph, until they have established the most effective proportions of the picture. These they mark with a China marking pencil directly on the contact sheet or work print, which thereby becomes their guide when they make the final enlargement.

Cropping and section enlargement. Although it is always more advantageous to compose the picture in the viewfinder of the camera in such a way that the subject fills the entire frame, in practice this is not always possible. And even though certain photographers (for example, Henry Cartier-Bresson and W. Eugene Smith) allegedly never crop their pictures, this attitude seems to me to impose unnecessary restrictions on a photographer's work. I regard cropping during enlarging as a valuable tool of photographic creativity and, despite obvious shortcomings as a practical substitute for a moderate telephoto lens.

Cropping during enlarging consists of enlarging only a section instead of the entire negative, leaving out those marginal parts that contribute nothing to the characterization of the subject or may even affect it adversely. Undesirable picture matter of this kind may consist of an unsharp or meaningless foreground, objectionable forms intruding from the sides (branches, the corner of a house), utility wires crossing a corner of the sky, streaks of extraneous light from a light leak in the camera resulting in light-struck film, marks caused by uneven film development due to faulty agitation and so forth (p. 92). Another fault usually easily corrected during enlarging is a slanting horizon (the result of tilting the camera laterally), which should be made to appear horizontally in the print.

To find the most effective boundaries for their picture, knowledgeable photographers work with contact prints or the kind of work print described

Print proportions. By giving his enlargements proportions that are different from those of the negative, a photographer can further emphasize specific subject qualities and heighten the effect of the picture as demonstrated by these two versions of a truck stop in Nevada, both of which were cropped from the same square negative.

Print proportions. Under certain conditions, a photographer, by printing only a very narrow strip of a suitable negative, can give his picture the effect of an extreme wide-angle shot, as

above. With the aid of a pair of L-shaped pieces of cardboard placed together to form the boundaries of a variable rectangle, they mask the edges of the print, gradually decreasing the picture area within the enclosure formed by the two L's (while simultaneously trying out different proportions), until they have found the most effective way of cropping their picture. This they mark with a China marking pencil directly on the work print or contact sheet, which serves as their guide when they make the enlargement.

The limits of this method of print control are set only by the size of the negative section: the smaller the chosen section and the higher the degree of enlargement, the grainier and fuzzier the print. Whether or not the resulting degradation of print quality is acceptable is, of course, a decision every photographer must make himself.

In order to prevent stray light from further degrading the image quality of the print, a mask cut out of black paper (p. 52) must cover the entire negative except, of course, the part that is to be enlarged. In cases of extreme

demonstrated by this photograph of New York's
Hudson River waterfront which was made with
a standard Rolleiflex. A print of the entire negative is shown at the left.

scales of enlargement, this mask will also prevent light from the enlarger
lamp from passing through the edge of the negative, striking the chrome-
plated column of an enlarger with a vertical column, and reflecting onto
the print, where it would cause black, parabolic marks.

If the enlarger head cannot be raised sufficiently to achieve the desired
degree of magnification, one of four tricks may help. Exchange the regular
enlarger lens for one of a shorter focal length. If this is not feasible, rotate
the enlarger head around the column by 180 degrees, if possible, and place
the enlarger at the edge of the table and the easel on the floor, a box, or a
stool (instead of on the enlarger baseboard). Alternatively, if the design
permits this, rotate the enlarger head 90 degrees around a horizontal axis,
and project the negative on the wall to which the enlarging paper has been
fastened with adhesive tape. And if neither one of these devices is practical,
get yourself a 45-degree mirror of the kind made especially for this purpose
(consult the ads in the photo magazines), attach it to the enlarging lens,
and project the picture horizontally upon a wall with the enlarger head
remaining in its normal position.

Sectional enlargement of a suitable negative can substitute for a missing, moderate telephoto lens, as demonstrated by these views of Brooklyn Bridge in New York. *Above:* a print showing the negative in its entirety. *Opposite page:* an enlargement made from only a section of the same negative gives the impression of, and is indistinguishable from, a photograph made with a telephoto lens.

Cropping as a means for heightening the effect of a picture. *Above:* a print made from the entire negative. *Opposite page:* the carefully cropped, graphically condensed image which the author envisioned at the moment of exposure but was unable to get directly because, lacking a telephoto lens, he didn't dare to go closer for fear of alerting his subjects and running into trouble, or turning a candid "happening" into a stiff and posed picture.

Cropping as a means for saving a damaged negative: "crop" the ruined part and enlarge only the still-usable remainder.

Above: Salvaging part of a badly light-struck negative by cropping the worst of the stray-light damage and "burning in" (p. 100) the rest in order to save as large a part of the view as possible (*left:* the light-struck picture; *right:* the salvaged print). *Below:* By cropping the image of the photographer's arm which accidentally got in the way, at least part of a vacation shot of sentimental value could be saved.

**Overall contrast control
through paper gradation**

In addition to improving, in the print, the unsatisfactory gradation of a negative that is too contrasty or too "flat," papers of different gradation can also be used for deliberately increasing or decreasing the contrast of a "normal" negative. The accompanying illustrations show the same negative printed on soft, normal, and

Overall contrast control through paper gradation. The simplest method of controlling the gradation of a print is by printing the negative on paper of appropriate gradation (p. 33). If, when printed on paper of normal gradation, the print appears too contrasty, that is, dark areas are too black and devoid of detail, light areas are chalky white and lacking in differentiation, make a second print on paper of softer gradation. Conversely, if, when printed on paper of normal gradation, the picture appears too flat, that is, its darkest areas are dark gray instead of black, its lightest areas light gray instead of white, and its overall appearance soft and muddy, make another print on paper of harder gradation. If you work with variable-contrast paper (p. 37), try a darker or lighter filter in the appropriate color.

Overall contrast control through development. Notwithstanding the fact that best results are always achieved if the print has been developed normally (p. 45), in an emergency (for example, if a paper of the required gradation is unavailable or if only a slight change in gradation should be made—less than the step from one paper gradation to the next) a change

94

hard paper, each producing a somewhat different impression. Although these differences are slight—if they were greater, the effect would be unpleasant—they are significant. Experienced photographers take advantage of this form of print control where sensitivity is a prerequisite for success and heavy-handedness an invitation to disaster.

in the processing routine can substitute for a change in the gradation of the paper. Although the exposure latitude of photographic paper is very much smaller than that of film and furthermore varies with the kind of paper, a certain leeway exists, enabling a photographer to influence the gradation of his print by varying the time of exposure in conjunction with the time of development. To produce prints of softer gradation, slightly increase the time of exposure while decreasing the time of development. Conversely, to produce a print of harder gradation, slightly decrease the time of exposure while increasing the time of development.

Since different types of paper react differently, only tests can reveal how large these deviations from normal can be while still producing acceptable results. Furthermore, two precautions must be taken: The shorter the time of development, the more vigorously the print must be agitated during the entire development to avoid mottle or streakiness; and the longer the time of development, the more important it becomes to shield the developing paper from unnecessary safelight exposure in order to avoid fogging the print inadvertently. Incidentally, shortening the time of development usu-

Local contrast control (dodging). The principle: thin negative areas require less, and dense areas more, exposure than areas of intermediary density. *Above:* A "straight" or unmanipulated print from the abnormally contrasty negative shown *at the left*; shadow detail, although present in the negative (see the picture on p. 47, top), is absent in the print. *Below:* A correctly "dodged" print.

ally produces prints in warmer, more brownish tones than those characteristic of normal development, a fact which might or might not be an advantage.

Local contrast control through dodging—holding back and burning in (printing in). Rare indeed is the negative that can be printed straight, *i.e.*, whose contrast is so perfect that all its parts require exactly the same print exposure time. Usually, although overall contrast may be generally satisfactory, some negative areas would print too dark and others too light if the paper were given a uniform exposure during enlarging. For example, if the negative of a girl in a dark dress were exposed evenly during enlarging, either the face would appear in the print in the correct tone, but the dress would be too dark, or the dress would appear with satisfactory detail but the face would be too light. Printing such a negative on paper of softer gradation would, of course, lower the overall contrast sufficiently to reveal detail in both the face and the dress. Unfortunately, however, while decreasing the overall contrast to a printable level, this procedure would also lower the contrast within the face and within the dress to such a degree that both would appear too soft. The face would look grayish-white and pasty, the dress grayish-black and flat. In such a case, the only way of producing an acceptable print is by using a relatively contrasty paper and controlling negative contrast locally by holding back the dress and burning in the face, a process known as dodging.

Holding back means exposing the respective negative area for a shorter time than the rest of the picture. Conversely, burning in (or printing in) means exposing that negative area for a longer time than the rest of the picture. Technically, this is done by means of special dodgers (p. 30), although experienced operators work largely with their hands, forming the required shapes with their fingers.

Holding back. Negative areas requiring less exposure than the rest of the picture are shielded during part of the exposure either with a piece of cardboard interposed between paper and lens, or with the hand or hands. The shape and size of the cardboard depend on the shape and size of the area that has to be shielded, although a small piece of cardboard held relatively close to the enlarger lens does the same work as a larger piece held closer to the paper. To hold back relatively small areas, one requires a small piece of cardboard cut roughly to the appropriate shape of the area that is to be held back and fastened to the end of a stiff wire serving as a handle. The *effective* shape and size of this dodger (actually, the form of its shadow on the photographic paper) can, of course, be varied to a considerable degree by tilting it more or less on edge (which makes the shadow narrower)

Local contrast control (dodging):
the fine points

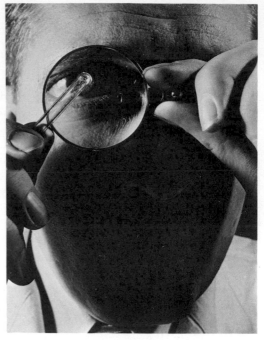

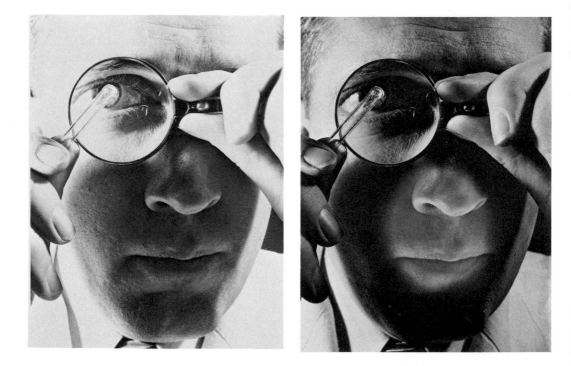

Proper blending of dodged and undodged areas is essential for a natural appearing print. *Opposite page, top left*: The negative—abnormally contrasty—showing a scientist examining a vial of synthetic penicillin. *Top right*: A "straight" print; selection of an exposure long enough to bring out detail in the dense areas of the negative yielded a picture in which the shadows appear too black. *Bottom left*: Conversely, an exposure appropriate to maintain satisfactory shadow detail resulted in a picture in which the lighter areas appear unnaturally light. *Bottom right*: Faulty dodging left a ring of darkness around a shadow area held back too much and therefore appearing unnaturally light. *Above*: A correctly dodged print, characterized by adequate detail in both highlights and shadows; transition between the light and dark areas is inconspicuous and appears natural.

and holding it closer to or farther away from the lens (which increases and decreases, respectively, the size of the shadow on the print). An indispensable prerequisite for effective dodging is moving the dodging device continuously with an irregular, fluttering, or more or less concentric motion, as the case may be; otherwise, the dodged area would be surrounded by a more or less sharply defined, lighter or darker edge, and the wire handle would cast a shadow that would appear in the print as a light and slightly fuzzy streak.

Burning in (printing in). Negative areas requiring more exposure than the rest of the picture are given additional exposure with the aid of a "negative" dodging device, a sheet of cardboard with a hole in the middle or an opening formed by the hands. The latter method has the advantage that the aperture can be varied instantly in both size and shape in accordance with the form of the area to be printed in. As in the case of holding back, the size and shape of the opening through which the overly dense negative areas receive additional exposure can be varied in both respects by working at a greater or lesser distance from the lens and by tilting. To avoid surrounding the treated area with an unsightly ring or "halo", the hands or card must be kept in roughly circular or fluttering motion throughout the entire procedure.

General advice. Dodging as a means of print control is satisfactory only if it is unnoticeable in the print. Therefore, when burning in an area, make sure that the light does not spill over into adjacent parts of the picture; otherwise it would form a dark zone of transition between the treated and the untreated parts. On the other hand, do not constrict your burning in activity too much either, because this would produce a dark center within the treated area. If holding back is required, shade the area in question evenly and not too much; overdoing the shading would produce a grayish area which, in comparison to the rest of the picture, would appear unnaturally light.

If a straight print appears unsatisfactory, study it carefully in regard to contrast distribution before you attempt a dodged one. Sometimes, particularly if the areas requiring dodging are numerous, it is better to switch to a paper of softer gradation. However, keep in mind that many negatives are simultaneously too hard and too soft, unlikely as this may sound. In backlighted scenes, for example, contrast between light and shadow may be extreme, but *within* the light and the dark areas themselves, contrast is usually very low. Printing such a negative on paper of soft gradation would only yield a print in which the highlights appear muddy-gray and the shadow areas flat. In such a case, paradoxical as it may sound, the only way to get a decent print is to use a paper of *hard* gradation, hold back the shadows, and burn in the highlights, regardless of the fact that the amount of dodging required can be staggering.

To be able to reprint a difficult negative without having to waste time and paper on new test prints, many photographers make notes on the dodging procedure, drawing a rough diagram of the dodged areas either directly on the back of the print, on a separate piece of paper, or on a file card, and writing the applicable exposure times in the appropriate places, as well as the f/stop number of the enlarger lens and the make and gradation of the paper. Such a diagram might look like this:

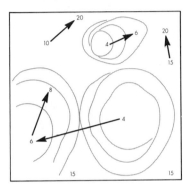

To print in very small areas, make yourself a dodger by poking the point of a ballpoint pen through a sheet of cardboard, then use it to shade the paper while exposing the small, overly dense negative area through the tiny hole.

Avoiding conspicuous light or dark haloes around dodged areas is easier if the dodger—whether a piece of cardboard on a wire or a hole—is cut with a jagged, toothed, or feathered edge instead of a straight one.

To blend the treated area with its surroundings instead of moving the dodging device in the horizontal plane, you can also move it vertically up and down. Either way, the right kind and amount of motion—neither too little nor too much—is a matter of experience and practice.

For the most precise dodging, work as closely as possible to the paper and use a correspondingly large dodging device. In cases where it is particularly important that the treated and untreated areas blend unnoticeably, work as closely as possible to the lens, and instead of a cardboard dodger, use one consisting of a fluffy piece of absorbent cotton stuck to the end of a wire.

To improve the accuracy of their work, for better visibility, and to avoid inadvertently fogging their paper, experienced photographers turn off the safelight during an extended dodging operation.

Local contrast control (dodging). Which paper gradation is best? The negative which yielded these pictures belongs to that rather common kind which, at the same time, is too contrasty and too flat. Too contrasty in so far as contrast between ground and sky is abnormally high; too contrastless because, *within* the area of the ground as well as *within* the area of the sky, contrast is abnormally low.

When faced with such a negative, inexperienced photographers automatically reach for a paper of soft gradation, their minds reacting to the stimulus "high contrast" with the response "soft paper." Unfortunately, the result would be a print like the one at the top of the opposite page which, despite the fact that it contains detail in both ground and sky, makes a flat and "muddy" impression. On the other hand, making a "straight" print on a paper of hard gradation does not solve the problem either but would only produce a picture like the one shown at the left.

The only way to get a satisfactory print from a negative in which contrast is at the same time too high and too low is to use a paper of relatively *hard* gradation and overcome excessive contrast by means of dodging. In this case, giving the ground a relatively short and the sky a relatively long exposure resulted in the print reproduced *above* which, in my opinion, gives a representative impression of this Western landscape.

103

Lightening areas that are too dark. When in doubt, printing certain negatives areas too dark is better than printing them too light. Once the print is in the fixer, there is nothing anybody can do about an area that is too light; but you can always make a dark area appear lighter by reducing its density with a ferricyanide solution. This is done as follows:

Prepare the reducing bath by pouring a small amount of red ferricyanide crystals into a 5" x 7" *white* tray; then add water, and stir until the crystals are dissolved. Concentration is right if the bath has a strong light yellow color. If it is dark yellow or orange, add more water; if it is a very pale yellow, add more crystals; if in the process of reducing, it turns greenish, it is exhausted and must be replaced by a freshly prepared bath. Textbooks always give exact measurements in ounces of crystals per ounces of water; in my experience, this is unnecessary since the concentration of the bath is not critical and its color instantly indicates whether its composition is right. Furthermore, contrary to the textbooks, I never add hypo to the solution because this would decompose it too soon. Instead, I suggest you proceed as follows:

Take the print out of the fixer, and place it emulsion side up on the bottom of an overturned tray in the sink. Take a tuft of absorbent cotton, dip one corner in the ferricyanide solution, squeeze it slightly to prevent fluid from dripping during the transfer to the print, then slowly swab the area that is too dark for a few seconds, being *very* careful neither to stray outside the area that is to be treated nor to drip ferricyanide solution on the print, since this would cause indelible spots immediately and instantly ruin the print. *Do not swab* until the treated area is as light as you want it to look, because, in that case, it would probably appear too light when dry, since ferricyanide keeps on acting until it has been completely neutralized by hypo. Therefore, shortly *before* the treated area appears just right, transfer the print *quickly* back to the fixer, and agitate it *vigorously* for 10 to 15 seconds. Then take it out, place it on the display panel (p. 71), and inspect it. If it is still too dark, repeat the performance until the desired degree of reduction has been achieved. Otherwise, leave the print in the fixer for a few minutes, then continue processing as usual.

Print-reduction with ferricyanide is an art about which some authors have written entire chapters. Actually, controlling print contrast with ferricyanide is not half as difficult as it sounds, provided the operator rigidly adheres to the following simple but vitally important rules:

Reducing density with ferricyanide is an irreversible process. Once overdone, the print is ruined. Therefore, proceed with extreme caution, go slowly, work in steps, go back and forth between reducer and fixer, check and inspect constantly, always keeping in mind that, as long as the area in question is still too dark, there is hope; once it is too light, you have lost the print.

Ferricyanide continues to lighten the image until it is either exhausted or neutralized by hypo. Therefore, stop the treatment shortly *before* the treated area has reached the desired degree of lightness, because otherwise, during the moment of transfer to the hypo, it may already have turned too light.

Be extremely careful not to take up too much ferricyanide solution with your cotton tuft. If the solution is allowed to run beyond the treated area, or to drip anywhere onto the print, indelible spots will result virtually at once, and the print will be ruined.

Density-reduction takes place through *chemical* reaction; it is *not* a mechanical process. Therefore, rubbing and grinding will not accelerate the reduction process but only scuff the emulsion. In other words, work very lightly.

As in dodging (p. 97), it is important that the treated area blends unnoticeably with its surroundings. To accomplish this, work the cotton tuft with a more or less circular motion—the circles expanding and contracting slightly as you go—*without* going beyond the treated area to such an extent as to produce a lighter halo, nor staying too long near the middle and thereby turning its center into a noticeably lighter spot. Successfully blending the reduced and unreduced areas of a print is the most difficult part of chemical reduction and can be learned only through practice. My advice: Practice on some discarded prints, until you acquire the necessary degree of skill before you try your hand on a good print.

To treat large print areas, use a fistful of cotton; for medium-sized areas, use proportionately less. For small areas, I found Q-Tips very practical. For minute areas like, for example, the catchlights in the eyes, use a fine watercolor brush; be careful to barely touch its tip to the surface of the print, because, if you press down on it, the point will spread and instead of a dot you will produce a blob.

Although it is most convenient to reduce prints immediately after fixing, dry prints can be treated, too: Soak the print in water for about 20 minutes, then proceed as described above.

Print-reduction is not limited to the treatment of specific areas. A print that is generally too dark can also be made lighter with ferricyanide, although, in my opinion, it is normally simpler to make a new print. But if the print is very large, or was difficult to make in the first place, reduction may provide a way to save it. The process itself is simple. Prepare a *very weak* solution of ferricyanide. It should be *very pale* yellow. If the print was dry, soak it first for 20 minutes in water; otherwise, take the print out of the fixer, rinse it briefly, then immerse it quickly and evenly in the ferricyanide bath. Agitate continuously with a gently rocking motion, alternating between side to side and front to back movements, for five or *at the most ten seconds*; then transfer the print quickly back to the hypo, agitate for 10 to 15 seconds, place it on the display panel (p. 71), and inspect it. If it is still too dark repeat the performance, if necessary several times, always being careful not to overdo things, since this would mean the loss of the print. Also, be careful not to make the bath too strong because this would produce a permanent yellow stain in the print.

And finally a note of caution: Ferricyanide is a dangerous and potentially lethal poison. Treat it with respect, and keep it out of reach of children.

Darkening areas that are too light. If, after a full two minutes' development, some areas of the print are still too light while the rest, as far as overall density is concerned, appear satisfactory, a photographer has two choices: Either he can scrap the print and make a new one (this is normally the best course if the faulty print is relatively small and/or the unsatisfactory area considerably underexposed); or he can attempt to save the print by treating it with concentrated developer or hot water. The latter course is usually worth a try if the print is relatively large or was difficult to make because of extensive dodging, provided, of course, the degree of underexposure is not too serious.

The basis of these techniques is the fact that development can be speeded up (or forced) by two means: increasing the concentration of the developer, and increasing the temperature at which the reaction takes place. In practice, proceed as follows:

Pour some concentrated (undiluted) developer into a suitable vessel (like a small, squat jam jar), and keep it handy. Make yourself two or three swabs in different sizes by winding strips of cloth around the ends of wooden sticks and tying them securely with string. After the print has been fully developed, rinse it briefly, and place it emulsion side up on an overturned tray in the sink, dip a swab of suitable size into the concentrated developer, and wait until it stops dripping. Then touch it lightly to the print area that appears too light, using the same circular movements and taking the same precautions against dripping and running as recommended for print reduction with ferricyanide (p. 104). Continue until the area has darkened sufficiently, if necessary repeatedly applying fresh developer concentrate, but always being careful that the solution neither drips nor runs into adjacent areas, because this would cause dark streaks and spots. If the area that is to be treated is very small (for instance, faces in a crowd), use a small Q-Tip dipped in concentrated developer instead of a big cotton swab. When the desired degree of darkening has been achieved, transfer the print to the acid stop bath, and continue processing as usual.

An alternative method for darkening specific print areas (which is particularly suitable for treating large areas like skies that turned out too light) is even simpler, involving nothing but hot water. In my own darkroom, where I have a stainless steel sink, I proceed as follows: With the aid of a short rubber hose attached to the faucet, I direct a stream of water as hot as I can get it onto a certain area in the sink, heating up the bottom. Then I quickly take the print with my hands by two adjacent corners, lift it out of the developer, and lower it onto the dripping wet, but *not* flooded sink bottom, letting only the part that is too light make contact with the sink. Alternatively, use the bottom of an overturned, heated up metal tray. Heat penetrating through the paper base will soon increase the activity of the developer taken up by the emulsion and adhering to the surface of the print, with the result that the area in question will begin to darken almost immediately. Care must be taken not to overdo the treatment, and the print should be returned to the developer *before* the desired degree of darkening has been achieved, since it will continue to darken for a while. If the first treatment does not produce the required effect, repeat the performance. On the other hand, if the print gets too dark, or if the effect accidentally spreads to adjacent areas, you can always try reduction with ferricyanide (p. 104); even if you do not succeed in saving the print, at least you get an opportunity to practice print-reduction with ferricyanide.

Lighter or darker prints? What constitutes the right degree of overall lightness or darkness in a print is a matter of personal opinion. A print some viewers consider just right will probably appear too light or too dark to others. But apart from subjective considerations, when calculating the exposure time for a print, photographers should keep in mind the following:

Simply by decreasing or increasing the exposure, a photographer can make the same negative yield a lighter or darker print. In other words,

Lighter or darker print?

Through appropriate changes in exposure time, a photographer can, at will, produce lighter or darker prints from the same negative. Normally, the acceptable range between light and dark is relatively small (as in the series shown here)—heavy-handedness leading to pictures which look either "washed out" (if too light) or "muddy" (if too dark). In this connection, an interesting phenomenon can be observed: if shown two "acceptable" prints, one lighter, the other darker, an observer will almost invariably decide that an intermediate version would be still better; and out of a series of three pictures of varying degrees of lightness, he will pick the one in the middle as "the best," even if he would pronounce the lighter or the darker version "excellent" if he saw it alone. And the same would probably happen if three prints in varying degrees of contrast were judged: unless the variations are extreme, chances are overwhelming that the intermediate version would be preferred.

he has a choice—an opportunity to control the effect of his picture. In this respect, experience has shown that lightness suggests happiness, youth, and femininity, and evokes joyful and positive feelings; conversely, darkness suggests seriousness, power, masculinity, old age, drama, tragedy, and generally creates a more somber mood. Often, it is astonishing how great the difference in feeling between a lighter and a darker print made from the same negative can be, and although it sometimes may be difficult to say which of the two is better (both may be good, each in its own way), at other times one is clearly preferable to the other. Therefore, many photographers make it a habit never to make only a single print from an important negative; instead, they make several with slightly different exposure times and afterwards select the one that makes the strongest impression. Experimentation improves their chances for success.

Lighter or darker print? Three negatives—six prints, **six** different impressions. Often, it is impossible to decide whether the lighter or the darker version of a specific subject is "better" because both can be "good," each in its own way. One may have qualities which the other lacks while the second may have something to offer which is missing in the first— for example, clarity of shadow detail in one as opposed to graphic con-

trast, power and strength in the other. Experienced photographers know
that of two different prints one must not necessarily be *better* than the
other. Therefore, to extract the maximum value from their negatives, they
usually are not satisfied with only one "good" print, but make several in
different degrees of lightness. Later, they leisurely pick the one which
they consider "the best."

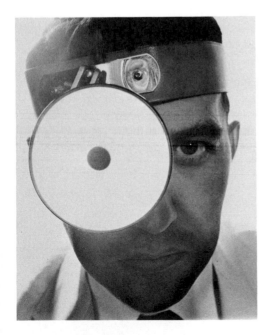 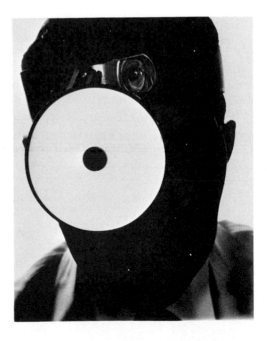

High-key or low-key? Two solarized versions derived from the
same negative, printed on paper
of hard gradation, are given great-

High key and low key. Not every subject is suitable for rendition in a full
range of tones. Some, like certain female nudes, portraits of girls and young
women, or scenes bathed in brilliant light, are most compelling if treated
in a light and delicate manner; others, like certain masculine portraits, subjects suggestive of power, dramatic scenes, and pictures of serious or somber
events, require darkness for strongest emotional effect. In such cases, creative photographers turn to the techniques of high-key or low-key printing
for achieving their goal.

High-key printing. Prerequisite for success is a shadowless rendition,
either by means of frontal illumination or by indirect light resulting in a
negative of *lower* than average contrast. Printing can be done in one of two
ways: (*1*) Use a paper of very soft gradation, give about twice the normal
exposure, then develop in a highly diluted developer—"highly" here mean-
ing from five to ten times the regular amount of water added to the de-

er emphasis by means of high-key and low-key printing, respectively. "Straight" prints of the two negatives are shown in smaller scale for comparison.

veloper concentrate. The developing time, of course, must be increased accordingly. Should a particular developer react with yellow stain, add 3 to 4cc of a developer-improver such as Latitol U, Johnson 142, or Ilford IBT per 1000cc of working solution. *(2)* Use a paper of very hard gradation, expose on the short side, develop somewhat longer than normal in any standard paper developer. In comparison with the first method, the effect will be harsher and more graphic, more modern in feeling, less soft. The best way to decide which of the two is more suitable in a given case is to try both. However, either way, making a successful high-key print is not easy and is rarely accomplished on the first try.

Low-key printing, to be successful, requires a paper of relatively hard gradation in conjunction with a longer than normal exposure and full development. Black shadows devoid of detail can be an asset rather than a fault. The idea is to strive for a powerful graphic effect rather than merely a darkened naturalistic impression.

Two studies of the nude by *John Veltri*. Printed from ordinary, sharp negatives, both derive their special effect from a deliberate softening of their outlines during enlarging. In the case of the picture above, the lens was deliberately adjusted for out-of-focus projection. The picture on the opposite page was softened by "zooming"—by gradually changing the focus of the enlarger lens during the exposure of the paper.

Softening through diffusion. A soft-focus effect can be produced either directly in the negative (by shooting the picture through a diffuser), or afterwards in the print. Although, at first glance, the results may seem similar, they are subtly different. In the first case, the highlights spread into the shadows; in the second case, the shadows spill over into the lights. And

while the first effect is unquestionably preferable, it involves the disadvantage that diffused negatives can never yield sharp prints, whereas any sharp negative can be made to yield not only prints that are diffused in different ways but, should diffusion prove after all to be not such a good idea, also prints that are sharp. Furthermore, should a photographer wish to get the first-mentioned diffusion effect from a sharp negative, all he has to do is to photograph a sharp print made from this negative through a diffuser; ordinary prints made from the resulting copy negative will then show a diffusion effect indistinguishable from what would have been created if the negative had been diffused while making the shot.

Diffusing is a technique that positively invites misuse, particularly if it is employed to obliterate the lines and wrinkles in a face engraved by age —the markings that give character to a face and without which it would lose its identity—the record of a lifetime blurred or wiped out by a thoughtlessly applied technique. On the other hand, diffusing can heighten the effect of the picture in cases in which a photographer wishes to create a soft and romantic mood—vapors rising from a river in the early morning with the sun trying to break through the mist . . . or the vision of a nude bathed in shimmering light. . . .

During enlarging, a picture can be diffused in several ways: (1) by throwing the image out of focus; (2) by placing a diffuser between the enlarger lens and the paper. Special glass diffusion disks are available in photo stores which slip on the lens like a filter. There are several materials suitable for use as home-made diffusers. A sheet of thin, transparent acetate, for example, one of the sleeves used to protect color transparencies, if first crumpled and then straightened, will produce a stronger diffusion effect than while it was still smooth. A piece of nylon fabric such as a ladies' stocking, preferably dark or black, will also do nicely. In either case, the degree of diffusion can be varied by varying the distance between diffuser and lens: the closer to the lens, the more diffused the print, and vice versa. (3) Diffusing the image during only part of the exposure, resulting in superimposition of a sharp and a diffused image, can lead to particularly interesting effects.

Photographers interested in diffusion effects should experiment with the different techniques described above and also try other kinds of diffusers (metal or nylon fly screens, different kinds of "antique" or pebble glass and so on). Under certain conditions, moving the diffuser during the exposure like a dodger (p. 100) may be necessary for achieving the desired effect.

Diffusion reduces contrast, sometimes to a considerable degree. Consequently, a negative that is to be diffused must normally be printed on paper of a gradation that is one or two steps *harder* than would ordinarily have been used.

A somewhat different diffusion effect can be achieved with the aid of petroleum jelly (Vaseline) smeared on a sheet of glass interposed between the enlarger lens and the paper. This technique lends itself to considerable variation. A thin film of jelly, for example, provides a mild diffusion effect, a heavier coating a stronger one. Coating only the edges of the glass with jelly while leaving the middle clear results in a picture in which the central area is rendered sharp, while subject matter near the edges appears diffused, if necessary, to the point of total blur.

Correcting perspective distortion. In photography, one of the manifestations of perspective is the fact that parallel lines that recede from the camera are rendered in the form of converging lines. As long as such parallel lines occur in the horizontal plane (like, for example, railroad tracks or the horizontal lines of buildings), this phenomenon appears not only perfectly normal in the picture, but even desirable as a means for graphically creating the illusion of depth. And the more abrupt the degree of convergence (wide-angle perspective!), the stronger the feeling of depth.

Unfortunately, this no longer holds true if the receding parallels are *verticals*, the convergence of which is usually felt to be unnatural. For example, in photographs of buildings taken with the camera tilted upward, vertical lines converge toward the top of the picture, thereby creating in most viewers' minds the impression of structures on the brink of collapse. Similarly, in commercial photography, the picture of, say, a book or a box of cereals, is supposed to show the sides of the subject rendered parallel, even though the view may have been taken from above and a certain amount of convergence toward the bottom of the picture would have to be expected. Such unwanted convergence of actually parallel lines can be corrected in the print either by making the picture with a view camera equipped with swings (instructions for this are given in the author's books, *The Complete Photographer* and *Total Picture Control*), or by compensation during enlarging.

To correct the convergence of actually parallel lines with the aid of an enlarger, the distorted negative must be projected relative to the paper at such an angle that perspective compensates for distortion. This is precisely the reverse of the process that caused the distortion in the first place—the fact that, say, the lower part of a building was closer to the lens than the upper part and was rendered correspondingly larger. Now, if we arrange negative and paper relative to one another in such a way that the top of the building is enlarged proportionally more than the bottom, the verticals will be restored to the parallel in the print.

Theoretically, lines that converge in the negative will be restored to the parallel and the print will be *sharp in its entirety*, if the negative, the lens and the paper are arranged in such a way that imaginary lines drawn through their planes intersect in a common point. To achieve this, negative and paper must be tilted relative to one another and the lens as shown in the diagram below:

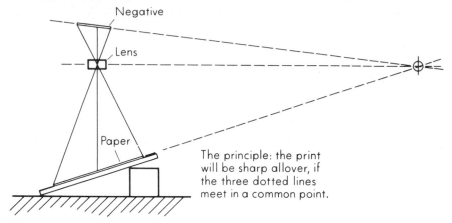

The principle: the print will be sharp allover, if the three dotted lines meet in a common point.

How this can be accomplished *in practice* depends on the design of the enlarger (p. 26). If the enlarger features either a tilting negative carrier (the best solution), a tilting enlarger head, or a tilting lens stage, the problem is simple and can easily be solved in accordance with one of the following sketches:

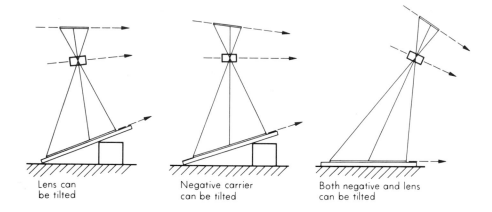

Lens can be tilted

Negative carrier can be tilted

Both negative and lens can be tilted

If neither one of these enlarger components is tiltable, try to tilt the negative as best you can by propping up one side with the aid of a make-shift support. If the enlarger design does not permit this, all you can do is to tilt the easel as much as necessary to achieve **parallelity of the vertical**

118

Correction of perspective distortion during enlarging. Step 1: A "straight" print from a "distorted" negative—vertical lines converge toward the top of the picture. To see how this very common but normally undesirable phenomenon can be corrected during enlarging, turn the page.

lines, focus on a point about one-third in from the raised edge of the paper, and stop down the lens until the entire print is sharp.

Since the upper and lower edges of the tilted easel lie at different distances from the enlarger lens, they receive different amounts of illumination. This would result in a print in which the top of the picture, which was relatively far away from the lens, is underexposed relative to the bottom, which was relatively close to the lens. To avoid this, the first must be given a proportionally longer exposure than the latter. This is easily done by dodging the print (p. 97) with a rectangular cardboard. To avoid streakiness, this dodger must be kept in constant fluttering motion during the gradual transit across the enlarger beam. The actual difference in exposure between the top and the bottom of the picture depends on the angle of the tilt—the steeper the tilt, the greater the difference—and must be determined with the aid of two test strips (p. 56), one at either end.

It goes without saying that, just as it is possible to eliminate certain forms of perspective distortion during enlarging, so it is also possible to increase distortion (perhaps to give additional emphasis to depth), and even to introduce deliberately distortion where none was present in the negative (perhaps to turn a portrait into a caricature). The possibilities in these respects are limited only by the imagination of the photographer.

Correction of perspective distortion during enlarging. Step 2: Tilt the paper until the converging verticals appear parallel again (*left*); the now trapezoidal picture will thereby be thrown partly out of focus. *Step 3:* Tilt the negative in the opposite direction until the picture appears sharp in its entirety (*right*); minor readjustments of focus may be required. *Opposite page:* The final, cropped, undistorted print.

PRINT CONTROL—IMPROVEMENT OR FAKE?

In addition to the print controls discussed on pp. 78–119, other techniques for influencing the appearance of a photograph exist which, in my opinion, should be avoided. Some, like printing through texture screens, introduce into the photograph a foreign element that I find objectionable. Others, like toning, vignetting, or elaborate black-border printing, seem to me misguided attempts on the part of the photographer to enhance his pictures with the aid of attributes popularly associated with painting in an effort to prove that Photography is Art; I find the resulting effects pitiful and ridiculous. Still others, like flashing or the use of new coccine, are of questionable value, difficult to use effectively and, in my experience, not

**Deliberate distortion produced
during enlarging**

This process is identical to that described and illustrated on pp. 117-121. *Above:* a print made from the original negative. *Opposite page:* the deliberately "distorted" print.

worth the effort. For these reasons, none of these techniques has been included in this guide.

As a matter of fact, the whole complex of photographic control is an extremely controversial subject. Techniques and effects that some photographers regard as legitimate forms of control are dismissed as faking by others. There is, of course, no way to draw an objective line between straight and controlled photography since even the most elementary decisions like, for example, which f/stop or shutter speed to use, are in the last analysis a form of control, since they influence the extent of depth of the sharply rendered picture zone or decide whether a subject in motion will be depicted sharp or blurred. Not to mention the fact that, whether or not we like it, any transformation of colorful reality into black-and-white photography implies control. To give a few examples: Does the picture of a landscape taken on orthochromatic film represent a straighter form of photography than a picture of the same landscape on panchromatic film merely because Brady, Atget, or any other of the "fathers of straight pho-

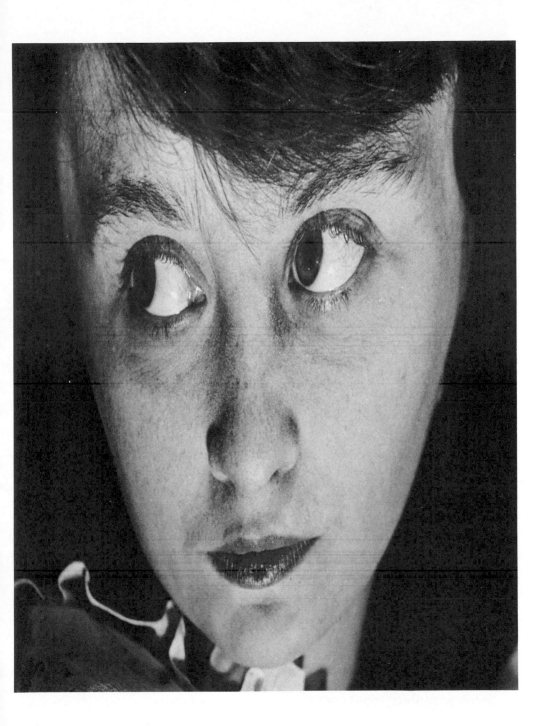

tography" worked with orthochromatic films? And what about the use of filters to improve (or falsify?) the rendition? Is an unfiltered photograph a more honest picture than a filtered one—even if this means a whitish sky whereas, actually, the sky was blue and enlivened by clouds (which a filter would have brought out in the picture)? And what about dodging? Burning in an overexposed sky, or holding back underexposed shadows— are these legitimate print controls designed to correct deficiencies of the negative or faking on the part of the photographer who subjectively must decide how far to go in these respects? But if filtering and dodging are legitimate, why not the use of blur as a graphic symbol of motion, since, for example, sharply rendered, the picture of an automobile in motion would be indistinguishable from that of an automobile standing still? Is the high-speed photograph of a splashing drop of milk an honest photograph or a fake, since obviously it shows an event in a form that does *not* conform to the way we see it in reality? But if this kind of picture, which renders the subject in a form that the eye cannot see directly, is accepted as legitimate, why not other forms of photographic rendition? Like, for example, cylindrical and spherical perspectives, familiar to all through pictures made with panoramic cameras or fisheye lenses; or photographs taken with extreme wide-angle or telephoto lenses, whose perspectives are popularly considered distorted (a fallacy, as I explain in my book *Photographic Seeing*); or photomacrographs showing tiny objects enlarged to many times their natural size and revealing aspects our imperfect eyes can never perceive without the aid of instruments? But if these kinds of photography —pictures that show objects and events in forms different from the ways in which we experience them in reality—are acceptable as legitimate, why not go all the way and use all the different devices and techniques that modern photography places at our disposal, with the aim of extending our visual experience to the limit?

It is in this spirit that I will discuss in the following chapter some of the techniques of *photo-graphic* print control, thereby giving the reader the means of extending the scope of his work into the realm of fantasy. All are strictly photographic insofar as they involve only the same devices and techniques as ordinary photography—no manual interference or manipulation as, for example, in bromoil-printing, no abrasion techniques, no drawing, painting, retouching, new coccine, and so on—nothing but the application of basic principles and standard techniques that by now should be familiar to the reader. But in contrast to the foregoing, where standard techniques were guided by standard rules, there are no longer any rules governing the applications of the means of photographic print control. Here, subjectivity reigns unchecked and creativity is king.

PHOTO-GRAPHIC PRINT CONTROLS

Multiple printing. A whole new world of fantasy opens up to the photographer who has the skill and the imagination to create his own images by combining two or more negatives in the form of one print. Phototechnically speaking, this can be done in one of two ways:

Combination printing with the aid of masks. This technique, which enables a photographer to combine elements of two negatives in one picture, is most often used to put clouds into a cloudless landscape photograph. This is accomplished in two steps: First, print the earth or foreground part of the picture (using negative A), while covering the part of the sensitized paper reserved for the sky with a cardboard mask; then print the sky part of the picture (using negative B), while covering the area of the paper imprinted with the foreground with a second cardboard mask.

To be able to produce a natural-appearing combination print, the photographer must watch out that its components match both aesthetically and phototechnically: aesthetically, in regard to direction of the light, perspective, composition, and general feeling and mood; phototechnically, in regard to contrast, *i.e.*, both negatives should require the same grade of paper. Otherwise, make the print on a variable-contrast type of paper, using one kind of filter for exposing the earth part of the picture, and another one for the sky.

Start composing your picture by placing the earth negative (negative A) in the enlarger and projecting it onto a sheet of ordinary white paper in the size of your future print. Select the degree of enlargement and cropping, in accordance with the requirements for the most effective composition. Trace the outline of the boundary between earth and sky on the white paper, using a hard pencil and working lightly since this outline may not be final and may have to be modified in accordance with the requirements of the cloud negative B. Remove negative A but leave the white paper on the easel.

Place the cloud negative B in the enlarger, and project it onto the white paper. By shifting the easel around and, if necessary, trying different degrees of enlargement, fit the clouds into the picture in such a way that foreground and sky form a compositionally satisfying unit. Sometimes flopping the cloud negative (reversing it in the negative carrier) will lead to a more satisfactory arrangement, and may even be necessary to make the illumination of the clouds appear to come from the same direction as the light that illuminates the foreground. Using a hard pencil, lightly outline the most important clouds on the white paper.

Combination printing. Left: A photograph of the Statue of Liberty in New York harbor —unsatisfactory because of its uninteresting "bald" sky. *Right:* The cloud negative which the author selected for this combination print because its dramatic upward sweep matches the raised arm of the Statue. *Opposite page:* The finished combination print.

Turn on the white light, and examine your sketch critically: Is the relationship of earth to sky satisfactory? Are the main picture components in harmony with one another? Would a shift here or a change there improve the balance of the picture? If the answer is yes, start all over again with negative A. But if you are satisfied, reinforce the main lines of your drawing by going over them with a soft lead pencil to produce a bold and clear outline guide.

Next, place the foreground negative in the enlarger, and adjust the projected image to fit your outline guide. Place a thin sheet of cardboard on top of the outline guide, and once more trace the boundary between earth and sky, this time on the cardboard. With a black felt-tipped marking pencil, write "earth" on the lower part and "sky" on the upper part of this mask; then cut the cardboard into two pieces along the skyline. Marking the two pieces of the mask will prevent possible confusion later by making it unmistakably clear which mask should cover the earth, which the sky, and which side of the cardboard is up.

With the aid of test strips (pp. 56, 58), determine the respective exposure times for the earth part and the sky part of your future picture. Each of the two negatives must, of course, be projected in the appropriate scale in

accordance with the outline guide. Be sure to develop both test strips together and for the same length of time—*not* one after the other. When they are fixed, evaluate the result in white light, and before you can forget them, write the respective *f*/stops and exposure times with pencil on the appropriate places in your outline guide. Having done this, you are ready to make the final print, proceeding as follows:

Place negative A in the enlarger, and project it in accordance with the outline guide. Take a sheet of enlarging paper, and mark on its back side which edge will form the top of the picture. Remove the outline guide from the easel. Insert the enlarging paper. Hold the mask marked "sky" close to the paper to protect the area that will subsequently be imprinted with the clouds, and turn on the enlarger light.

Expose the foreground in accordance with the test strip, shielding the sky area of the picture with the sky mask. Constantly vibrate back and forth in order to assure a proper blending of the tones of earth and sky in the print. This blending is the most difficult part of combination printing, because incorrect handling of the masks results in a transition zone that is either lighter or darker than the adjacent picture areas.

Having completed the exposure and turned off the enlarger lamp, put the sky mask away, hold an OA safelight filter in front of the enlarger lens, turn on the enlarger light, and using a Kodak negative pencil, mark the boundary between earth and sky with a few identifying dots applied in strategically important places. Be sure to place these dots inside the already exposed foreground area; otherwise, they will appear in the print as white spots. Although important as guides for the proper placement of the earth mask, these dots fulfill only a temporary function and must be rubbed off as soon as the print is in the developer.

Turn off the enlarger light. Take the paper off the easel and put it in a lighttight box. Put the outline guide back on the easel, and replace negative A with negative B. Adjust the scale of enlargement and position of the easel in accordance with the outline guide. Turn off the enlarger light, take the outline guide off the easel, and replace it with the pre-exposed sheet of paper, making sure (*1*) not to disturb the position of the easel, and (*2*) to place the paper with its "top" mark properly oriented. Hold the earth mask so that it shields the bottom part of the print, taking your cues from the row of identification dots made previously on the sensitized paper. Turn on the enlarger light, and expose the sky area of the picture in accordance with the test-strip data, being careful to vibrate the mask back and forth. Process the paper as usual, but do not forget to rub off the identification dots immediately upon immersion of the print in the developer.

128

Combination printing by the sandwich method. Two suitable negatives are placed in contact, emulsion facing emulsion, and enlarged together. The result, of course, is identical with that of a double exposure and will look like a mistake unless the photographer had a definite effect in mind and knew how to achieve it.

Alternatively, a negative and a photogram (p. 132) can be combined, or a negative and any object flat enough to fit into the enlarger, like a piece of lace, pressed leaves or flowers, a feather, a number of dandelion seeds, and so on. In any case, negative areas that are dark or black and objects that are opaque will appear light or white, and thin negative areas and translucent objects will appear dark or black in the print.

Somewhat different results can be achieved if the two negatives (or the negative and the flat object) are printed one after the other onto the same sheet of paper. In that case, interpenetration will be more complete, the effect more ghostlike, and freedom of creation greater, because different degrees of image magnification can be combined and exposures can be timed individually, making it possible to superimpose, for example, a strong image upon a faint one.

Quite different effects can be achieved if the flat object is first contact printed or enlarged on sheet film and the resulting negative combined with the other, normal negative of the sandwich. In such a case, the object will appear dark or black in the final combination print instead of light or white. And if a still more subtle effect is desired, the contact-printed negative of the object can be solarized (p. 140) before being superimposed on the image resulting from the normal negative.

Photograms. Place small objects with interesting outlines on a sheet of sensitized paper, and expose briefly with the enlarger lamp (without a negative in the enlarger). Then process as usual. The result will be a photogram—a shadowgraph of the object lying on the paper.

This simple technique of creating photographic images without a camera can be varied to an almost unlimited degree. Instead of using opaque objects, objects of different degrees of translucency, for example, can be used, yielding photograms in which the silhouettes are not harshly white and flat, but subtly modulated in graded shades of gray. Opaque objects can, of course, be combined with translucent ones for still more interesting effects.

Quite different images can be created by placing objects on a sheet of glass supported a certain distance above the sensitized paper in order to obtain more or less diffused silhouettes. This technique can be combined with the one described above for the production of images in which sharp

Combination printing. The purpose of this picture was to illustrate the spectacular height of the tide at Passamaquoddy Bay in Maine. To accomplish this, a rowboat was tied to a pier and photographed twice from the same camera position, first at high tide, then at low tide. Subsequently, the two negatives were printed together in the form of a sandwich.

Top left: The rowboat at high tide. *Top right:* The rowboat at low tide. *Left:* Print from negative No. 2 after modification that consisted of bleaching the upper part of the negative with ferricyanide to avoid possible double contours of the shack and pier in the background in case registration was not perfect during combination printing. *Opposite page:* The finished combination print.

Photogram. The simplest type of photogram (like the one shown here) consists of objects placed in direct contact with the sensitized paper which subsequently is briefly exposed to white light and developed. An enlarger is not required, although it provides a handy light source for making the exposure.

and unsharp forms interpenetrate. You may also modify the exposing light with the aid of filters of different textures such as rippled or pebbled glass. You can reflect light from differently curved, polished surfaces onto the sensitized paper or refract the exposing light with simple, differently curved positive or negative lenses (spectacle and desk magnifier lenses), prisms of various types, or other light-modulating devices.

Still more sophisticated photograms can be produced by using two or more light sources to create cross-shadow effects; by moving the light source during the exposure; or by exposing the paper at an angle instead of from above. Furthermore, through appropriate timing of the exposure, the background tone can be varied from deepest black to lightest gray, result-

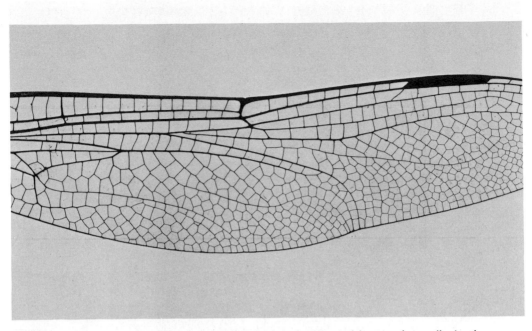

Direct projection. Objects of nature flat enough to be inserted in an enlarger (instead of a negative) are particularly suitable to direct projection—leaves, feathers, certain types of seeds or insect wings, and so on. This picture shows part of the wing of a dragonfly.

ing in more forceful or more delicate impressions. And by exposing the paper in a series of steps, the photographer can add or remove objects and thereby obtain overlapping silhouette effects in different shades of gray. Finally, the finished print can be used as a negative and contact printed onto another sheet of paper, producing a photogram in which the tonal values are reversed.

Direct projection. Another method of creating photographic images without a camera is by placing suitable objects in or on the negative carrier of an enlarger and projecting them onto sensitized paper. Since this technique circumvents the intermediate, image-degrading stage of the negative, sharpness and definition of the rendition are superb and enlargements are grainless, no matter how high the degree of magnification. Objects particularly suitable for this form of rendition are leaves, feathers, transparent insect wings, fish scales, and other small, flat, and more or less translucent objects of nature. Enlarged to many times their natural size, they can make breathtaking pictures.

133

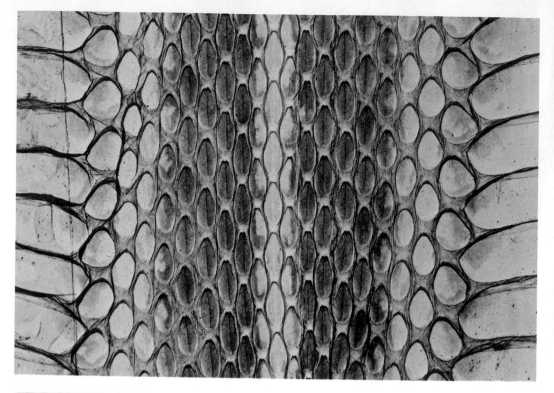

Direct projection in an enlarger. *Above*: Snake skin. *Left*: Milkweed seed. *Opposite page*: Flowering grasses. The graphic beauty of this kind of picture can be breathtaking.

Negative prints. Since black-and-white photography is already a semi-abstract medium of rendition, carrying this process one step further by turning positive images into negative ones does not seem such a farfetched idea. This can occasionally become desirable, because negative prints possess certain qualities not found in ordinary photographs: They are unusual—and the unusual always attracts attention; they permit dark subject areas and shadows to be rendered in much greater detail than in ordinary pictures; they accentuate the structural qualities of the subject by showing familiar objects in an unfamiliar form; they seem to turn day into night and ordinary objects into luminous, ghostly shadow-things glowing with a magic inner light. Photographers gifted with imagination and a feeling for graphic values will find in the negative process a method that enables them to realize certain kinds of vision and create a type of imagery in which fact blends with fantasy, resulting in pictures impossible to achieve by any other means.

Negative photographs are prints made from diapositives, and diapositives can be made in one of two ways: either by photographing a negative in transmitted light (on a light table or a sheet of backlighted flash-opal glass, with the negative carefully masked to prevent extraneous light from striking the lens); or by contact printing the negative on slow, orthochromatic film. In either case, the result would be a positive transparency, or diapositive. If such a diapositive is subsequently enlarged like an ordinary negative, the result will be a negative print.

Negative print of a paddle wheeler. Reversal of tone values turns an ordinary naturalistic photograph into a dreamlike vision—a river boat coming out of the night glowing with a magic, inner light.

Bas-relief. This technique permits a photographer to render his subject in a highly abstract form resembling woodcuts. To make a bas-relief print, you need a suitable negative and a diapositive contact printed from it. To be suitable, a negative must be critically sharp, relatively contrasty, and should contain only a few bold and interesting forms. In my opinion, harshly lighted nudes are particularly suitable for bas-relief rendition.

To make a bas-relief print, place the negative and diapositive together, emulsion facing emulsion. If you adjust the two in such a way that they are in register and examine them in transmitted light, you would see nothing but a uniformly gray or black surface since the positive half of this sandwich cancels out the negative half. But if you move them slightly out of register, lines will appear along the borders where light and dark tones met in the subject, forming a separate, graphic design. The width and relative positions of these lines can be controlled by varying the degree and direction of offset between negative and diapositive; normally, lines that are neither too narrow nor too wide will give the best effect. To get a pleasing design, work on a light table or slide-sorter by transmitted light, and try different degrees of offset in different directions. When satisfied, tape negative and diapositive together along their edges, place the sandwich in the enlarger, and make a print on contrasty paper.

Imaginative photographers will be interested to learn that the bas-relief technique allows for a number of variations. Varying the width and position of the resulting lines yields totally different effects, some of which will be better than others. Therefore, do not be satisfied with your first result, but try some variations. By varying the gradation of his paper, a photographer can produce bas-relief prints with or without intermediary shades of gray; usually, the pure black-and-white versions are better. And if the sandwich is enlarged on a piece of sheet film instead of paper, the resulting diapositive will yield bas-relief prints in which the tone values are reversed.

Bas-relief. This technique lends itself particularly well to the creation of bold and powerful, typically graphic effects. Its purpose is to convert a naturalistic rendition into a semi-abstract design.

Solarization.* This technique permits a photographer to render his subject in a highly abstract form resembling an etching. Unfortunately, it is also a very critical and somewhat unpredictable process that is difficult to control and, in the event of failure, ends with the destruction of the negative. It is therefore advisable to work only with expendable duplicate negatives, diapositives, or prints; the latter, which serve as negatives after they have been solarized, should not be smaller than 8" x 10".

Solarization is most effective when the subject is simple and bold, contrast high, and rendition critically sharp; low-contrast and fuzzy negatives and prints are totally unsuitable.

To produce a solarized print proceed as follows: Select a sharp and contrasty negative, and make an 8" x 10" enlargement on hard single-weight paper, exposing it in such a way that it can tolerate a two-minute development without turning too dark. When the paper is fully developed, while still in the developer, briefly expose it to white light, then continue the development. The fogged paper will, of course, rapidly turn black over its entire surface and must be transferred to the acid stop bath at precisely the right moment—the moment it has just turned black. Remove the paper too early, and solarization will be uneven and incomplete; remove it too late, and you are left with nothing but a uniformly black sheet of paper without the desired solarization lines. But if the duration of both the white-light exposure and the additional development was timed correctly, the fixed paper will show the boundaries of all the originally light subject forms delicately edged with fine, light lines, when examined in transmitted light. This solarized sheet of paper, fixed, washed, and dried like an ordinary print, subsequently serves as the negative from which the solarized print is derived by means of contact printing.

Because of the critical nature of the solarization process, good results can be expected only if the entire procedure is rigidly standardized on the basis of experiments and tests. Specifically, the wattage of the white light-bulb used for the second exposure, its distance above the developer tray, the time of the second exposure, and the duration of the subsequent development must be recorded to serve as the basis for corrections in case of failure, and in case of success to enable the photographer to repeat results.

---

* More precisely, the *Sabattier effect* or pseudosolarization. True solarization is the result of catastrophic overexposure, which, on film, produces a positive image. In photographs shot directly into the sun, for example, the disk of the sun is sometimes rendered black in the print due to solarization of the negative, in which the sun is rendered in positive form.

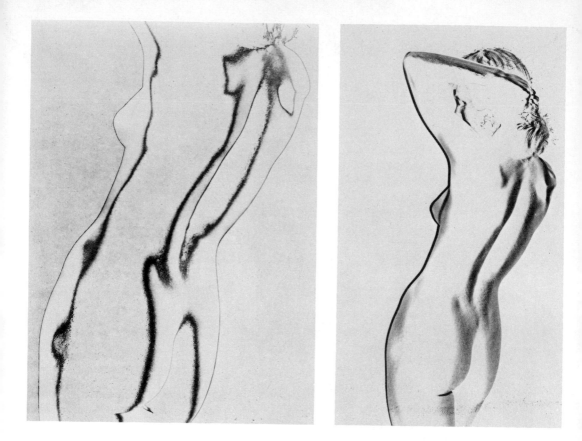

Whereas the dominant characteristic of a bas-relief print is strength, that of a solarized photograph is elegance. And although both techniques exploit the graphic effect of lines, there is a difference: lines created by means of bas-relief are broad and strong; those created by solarization are finely drawn, exquisitely precise, and often softly graded and "bleeding" into adjacent shades of gray. As a result, photographers sensitive to the potential of semi-abstract line renditions have the choice between strength and elegance.

These subtle differences are clearly illustrated by the comparison photographs on this spread. *Above left:* Solarization; *above right:* Bas-relief. Both pictures were printed on paper of extra-hard gradation to deliberately limit their tones to virtually pure black and white. In contrast, the solarized photograph on the *opposite page* was printed on a relatively soft paper in order to retain the texture of the paper negative.

142

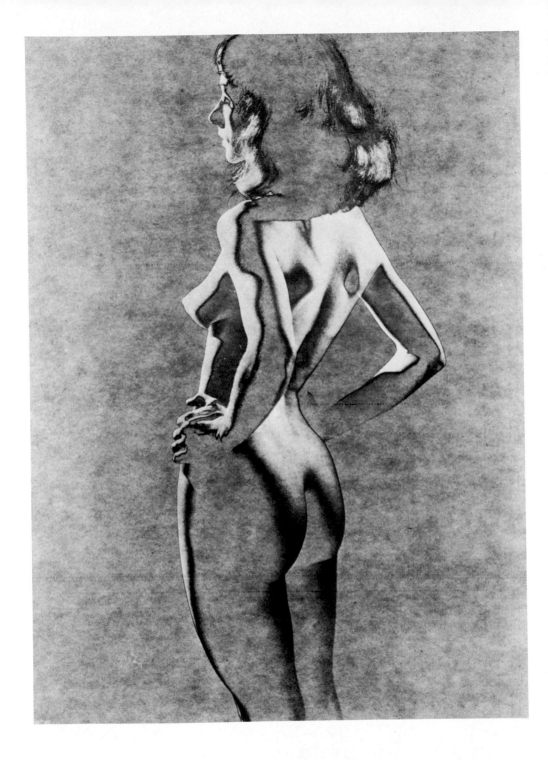

Reticulation. This technique permits a photographer to give his pictures a unifying surface texture producing a highly abstract, pointillistic effect of great expressive potential. Particularly suitable for this kind of treatment are negatives of relatively low contrast, which may be either sharp or blurred. High-contrast negatives usually produce disappointing results.

Negatives intended for reticulation should be hardened only moderately during fixation if the warm water treatment is going to be used, but may have been treated in an ordinary hardening fixer if they are going to be reticulated in a sodium carbonate solution. As far as subject matter is concerned, bold and simple forms invariably give better results than an overabundance of fine detail. Like the solarization process, the technique of reticulation is rather unpredictable and may end with the loss of the negative. Consequently, only expendable duplicate negatives or diapositives should be used. Prints do not reticulate.

To bring about reticulation, soak the negative in horizontal position in a tray of warm water, until the desired degree of reticulation has been achieved. The more prolonged the treatment, the coarser the grain. Then *without tilting*, which might cause the softened emulsion to flow, carefully transfer the reticulated negative to a tray filled with a hardening fixer at 65°F., where the soft emulsion will harden quickly and become suitable to normal handling. Wash and dry the negative as usual.

Since different emulsions react differently, the most effective water temperature must be established by test: Too hot, and the emulsion will melt and float off its base before reticulation sets in; too cold, and reticulation will be uneven or incomplete, or will not set in at all. The process of the reticulation effect can be checked visually (preferably, in a clear glass tray illuminated from below to show the negative in transmitted light) and must be stopped before the emulsion begins to split, frill along the edges, and melt and flow off its base.

Alternatively, a negative can be reticulated by treating it in a 10% solution of sodium carbonate at 125°F. This method has the advantage of avoiding excessive softening of the emulsion, which, after the desired degree of reticulation has been achieved, can be hardened simply by transferring the negative to a tray of cold water.

Reticulation. Whereas bas-relief and solarization create specific *line-effects*, reticulation achieves its characteristic effect by means of a unifying *overall pattern* not unlike that produced with the aid of texture screens. But whereas a texture screen arbitrarily superimposes an artificial design upon a photograph, the grain of reticulation organically evolves out of the design of the picture itself.

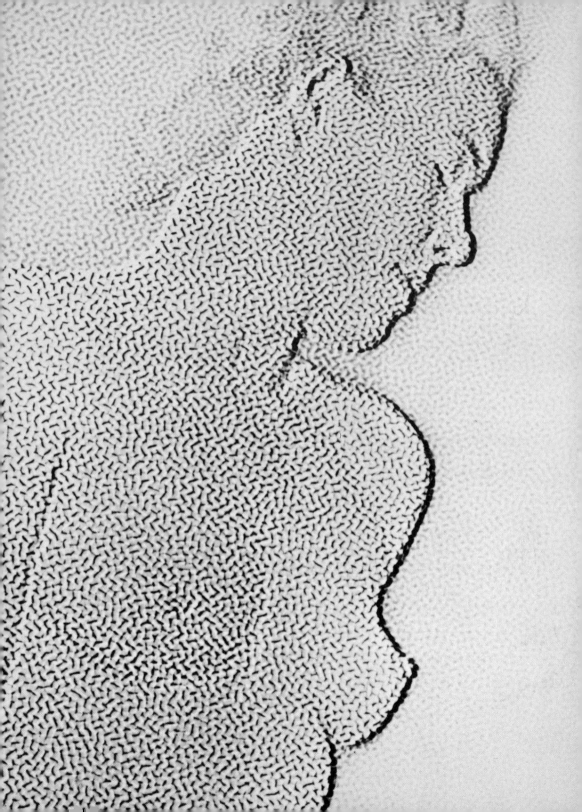

Combinations. A priceless bonus for the creative photographer is the fact that two or more of these photographic processes can be combined to produce still more sophisticated results. For example, to make a negative print, a photographer must first contact print a negative on film to produce a diapositive. A print made from such a diapositive would, of course, yield a negative picture. Subsequently, this same diapositive, in conjunction with the original negative, could be used to produce a bas-relief print. Alternatively, projected onto film instead of paper, a bas-relief negative can be created, which, when printed, would yield a negative bas-relief print. Such a negative bas-relief print could in turn be solarized and used as a paper negative from which solarized bas-relief prints can be made by contact printing. Or a duplicate negative can be reticulated, the reticulated negative contact printed on film, and the two used together to make a reticulated bas-relief print. If used as a paper negative, this reticulated bas-relief print could then be used to produce reticulated bas-relief prints in which the tone values are reversed. Or a straight negative can be combined with a reticulated diapositive to yield a semireticulated bas-relief print. Such a print could then be solarized, used as a paper negative, and contact printed to yield a semireticulated solarized negative bas-relief print. And so on. The possibilities are limited only by the imagination, patience, and time of the photographer.

Combination print derived from a "sandwich" consisting of an ordinary negative and the reticulated diapositive made from it. Reticulation, like an organic texture screen, gives the picture a feeling of graphic unity; the bas-relief effect, by emphasizing the outline, gives it strength.

148

Variations of a theme. *Top row:* 1—Print made from the direct projection of a leaf on film. 2—Print from a diapositive made from No. 1. 3—Bas-relief print derived by combining Nos. 1 and 2 and printing them, slightly off register, in the form of a "sandwich." 4—Print made from the solarized diapositive of No. 3.

Bottom row: 5—Solarization of the original negative. 6—Solarization of the diapositive derived from the original negative. 7—Double solarization produced by solarizing negative No. 5.

Solarization of a direct projection of leaves.

150

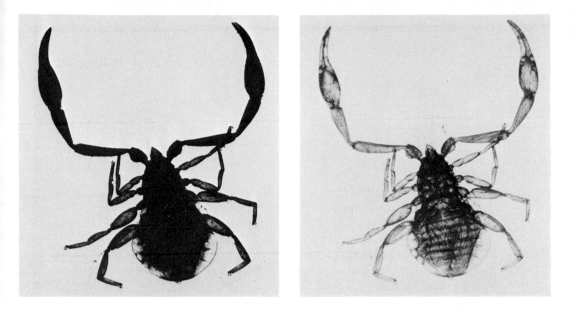

Variations of a theme. Direct projection of a tiny insect magnified here about 12 times linear. *Top left:* Projection on orthochromatic film produced hardly more than a silhouette. *Top right:* Projection on infrared film clearly shows most of the internal structure of this tiny creature. *Bottom left:* Reversal into the negative form improves the clarity of the rendition. *Bottom right:* Combining the second and third shots by the bas-relief technique produces the most informative picture and an almost three-dimensional effect.

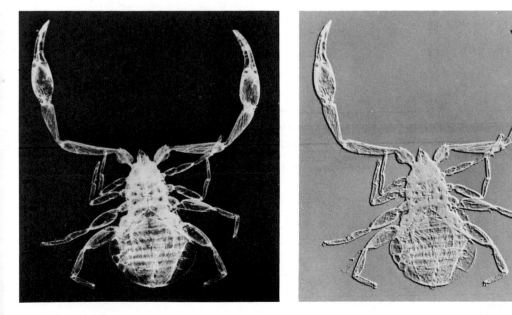

V. How to avoid mistakes

Throughout this book, I have tried to tell the reader how he can avoid making mistakes. In the following, I wish to add a few observations about mistakes in general.

It has been my experience that every mistake a photographer makes can be a blessing in disguise, provided, of course, the perpetrator is aware of it and sufficiently interested in his work to find the underlying cause. Once he has made a certain mistake, discovered its cause, and learned how to avoid it, he never has to make the same mistake again. We therefore arrive at conclusion number one:

Seen and evaluated as a profitable experience, every mistake a photographer made can be a milestone on the road to perfection.

Photographic materials made by reputable manufacturers are generally of such high quality and uniformity that failure due to manufacturing defects are extremely rare, provided the photographer followed the applicable instructions for use. Out of hundreds of faulty photographs I have seen, only a handful of the defects were caused by the manufacturer; the rest of the problems were due to mistakes on the part of the photographer who disregarded instructions. Consequently, here is conclusion number two:

Carefully read and follow the instructions for use which accompany every piece of photographic equipment and package of photographic material.

Before you blame disappointing results on the manufacturer of your photographic equipment or material, retrace your steps and make a real effort to find out what went wrong; the chances are overwhelming that the fault was yours. But if you are really stymied, Kodak provides a service for users of its products which might be able to help you. Send the puzzling pictures together with their negatives and an explanatory letter to the following address, and you will receive an authoritative reply free of charge:

Sales Service Division
Eastman Kodak Company
Rochester, N.Y. 14650

Product Services Dept., Kodak Ltd.,
Station Road, Hemel Hempstead,
Herts HP1 1JU.

Whereas stupid people try to forget their mistakes, smart ones try to remember them in order to avoid repeating them in the future. Smart photographers, instead of relegating every faulty negative or print to the waste can, save the more unusual and informative ones and file them together with their data for future references. In this way, they gradually build up a priceless reference library of unpleasantnesses to avoid and methods of avoiding them. They reason that they paid for these mistakes with their money, work, and time, so they may as well reap the benefits. And so we arrive at conclusion number three:

Save interesting and informative photographic mistakes in the form of ruined negatives and prints so that you and others can profit by them.

Unfortunately, in photography, most mistakes are final. Few can be corrected, and most of these only incompletely. Which brings us to advice number four:

Avoiding photographic mistakes is simpler and cheaper, and pays off more often in the form of better pictures than trying to correct them.

While accidents can and do happen, the majority of photographic mistakes are due to one of three factors:

Carelessness
Forgetfulness
False economy

Carelessness manifests itself in many different forms, the most common ones of which are: fingermarks on negatives and prints (in the latter case, the result of handling sensitized paper with wet or hypo-contaminated

153

hands); sand inside the camera (the result of carelessness at the beach), causing scratches parallel to the edges of the film; dust that got inside the camera and settled on the film prior to exposure, manifesting itself in the form of white spots in the negative and black spots in the print; dust that settled on the film after development, showing up in the form of white spots in the print; unlabelled bottles and containers, leading to confusion and unnecessary mistakes; chemicals stored carelessly in paperbags, spoiling rapidly by taking up moisture from the air; carelessly spilled hypo solution, chemically contaminating an entire darkroom; manipulating photographic paper in the processing solutions by hand (instead of using print tongs), which is the most common cause of stained prints; guessing the temperature of processing solution or the time of development, leading to over- or underdeveloped films; fingernails kept too long, inviting ugly digs in still wet films; and absence of apron or towel in a darkroom or a dirty towel, an infallible sign of a photographer who does not care.

Forgetfulness can have rather disastrous consequences, most of which occur when taking the picture: forgetting to wind the film after each exposure when working with a camera in which winding the film and cocking the shutter are not mechanically coupled, leading to double exposure; forgetting to take off the lens cap—result: no picture; forgetting to pull the slide when working with sheet film or filmpack—result: ditto; forgetting to change the ASA film speed setting of the camera or exposure meter when switching to a faster or slower type of film—result: over- or underexposure; forgetting to change focus when changing from long shot to closeup or vice versa—result: unsharp pictures; forgetting to consider the filter factor when calculating the exposure of a shot made through a filter—result: underexposure; forgetting to consider the closeup factor when calculating a closeup exposure—result: ditto; forgetting to rewind 35mm film before opening the camera for reloading—result: catastrophically fogged film; forgetting to put away light-sensitive paper before turning on the white light in the darkroom—result: loss of the entire paper stock; and forgetting to clean the negative prior to enlarging—result: dirty prints.

False economy, instead of saving money, invariably leads to additional expenses, unnecessary waste, and avoidable disappointments; it manifests itself most often in the following forms: buying photographic equipment in the form of kits consisting of cheap and shoddy pieces not fit for children as toys (such kits must not be confused with the developing kits for color material, which, if made by reputable manufacturers, are of professional quality); buying an expensive camera but no exposure meter, resulting in faulty exposures and wasted film and opportunities; buying cheap unknown brands of photographic equipment, film, paper, or chemicals, of generally inferior quality; overworking processing solutions with resulting lowering of negative and print quality, increased danger of stain, and premature deterioration of the accomplished work; working with insufficient quantities of processing solutions, a common cause of streaks and stains in negatives and prints; and using a cheap, colored, unsafe lightbulb instead of a filter-equipped safelight.

HOW TO IDENTIFY THE CAUSES OF MISTAKES

Only mistakes whose causes are known can be avoided in the future. To be able to profit from his errors, a photographer must know what he did wrong. The following survey is an expanded recapitulation and at the same time a summary of things said elsewhere in this text:

Faults of the print that are NOT due to faults of the negative

Print generally too light: paper exposure too short (underexposure).

Print generally too dark: paper exposure too long (overexposure).

Print generally too contrasty: paper gradation too hard (too contrasty).

Print generally too contrastless: If the margins that were protected by the frame of the easel are white, the paper gradation was too soft, or the paper was accidently fogged while still on the easel. If the margins are gray instead of white, the paper was fogged either before or after it had been exposed on the easel. Most likely causes: stray light, safelight not really safe or too close to the paper, or outdated paper.

Print appears mottled in reflected light (wet or dry): Paper was over-exposed and taken out of the developer too soon in an attempt to prevent the print from turning too dark.

Print appears mottled, but only when viewed in transmitted light while still wet: acid stop bath too acid; fixer too strong or too acid; excessively prolonged immersion in the fixer. This fault is called "water-soak" and the affected print may eventually turn yellow.

Print has sharply delineated zones of different overall tones, and demark-ation lines are *never* perfectly straight: The paper was not immersed in the developer with one smooth motion. Islands temporarily sticking out of the developer received proportionally less development than the rest of the print and subsequently appeared in the form of lighter shades.

Print has sharply delineated zones of different overall tones, demarkation lines are *always* perfectly straight, and the print looks as if it was partly covered by a sheet of extremely fine ground glass: This effect is caused by another print sticking tightly to the affected print during the early part of fixation as a result of insufficient agitation.

Narrow, dark, short, irregular streaks resembling pencil marks, usually near the corners or edges of the print, are pressure marks caused by the print tongs, which bruised the emulsion. If you get these marks, cover the tips of your print tongs with short lengths of thin rubber hose.

Roundish or more or less elliptical marks consisting of concentric lines are Newton's rings—diffraction patterns that appear when film and glass pressure plates are not in perfect contact with one another. To avoid, either use a glassless negative carrier, or special anti-Newton's-ring glass pressure plates.

White fingermarks are the result of touching the surface of the paper prior to development with moist or hypo-contaminated hands.

White, hairlike spots are caused by dust or lint that settled on the negative *after* development.

Matte spots in the glossy surface of ferrotyped prints are caused by air trapped between the ferrotype plate and the print (p. 63).

More or less concentric cracks in the glossy surface of ferrotyped prints are the result of trying to remove the print from the plate before it was completely dry, of too hot drier temperature, or insufficient tension of the canvas apron that holds down the print.

Yellow or brownish, partial or overall stain in the print can be caused by any one of the following agents: exhausted developer; excessively prolonged development; exhausted stop bath; exhausted fixer; fixer contaminated with developer; prints sticking together in the fixer; insufficient washing; touching prints with developer-contaminated hands.

HOW TO CORRECT MISTAKES

As mentioned before, in photography, most mistakes are final, and although textbooks frequently give advice on how to correct disasters, most of these remedies are, at least in my opinion, not worth the effort. Therefore, in the following, I'll discuss only those salvage techniques which I myself find practical.

Whereas a negative is one-of-a-kind—an original—a print is one-of-many—a reproduction. Consequently, while it might conceivably be justified to go to considerable lengths trying to salvage an unsatisfactory negative, it is normally easier, cheaper, and less time-consuming to make a new print than to correct a defective one, provided, of course, that this is possible at all. In my experience, attempts to improve an unsatisfactory print are worth the effort only if the print is either very large or, because of complicated dodging, was difficult to make.

Prints that are too dark, either all over or in certain areas, can be lightened with ferricyanide. How this is done has been discussed on p. 104.

Intensification of prints that are too weak or too light is, in my opinion, a waste of time, although some authors recommend it. The best one can hope for is a brownish effect, which, to me, looks like mud.

Ferrotyped prints that show matte spots in their glossy surface can be refinished by soaking them for half an hour in water followed by re-ferrotyping, wherein the photographer must take care not to trap air between ferrotype plate and print. How this can be accomplished has been explained on p. 63.

Prints that dried buckling or were creased in the drier can be refinished by soaking them in water for half an hour and then drying them again, this time more carefully.

Prints that have spots caused by dust on the negative can be made spotless by spotting. How this is done has been explained on p. 64.

Print defects that cannot be corrected include the following: underexposure (print too light); excessive contrast; lack of contrast; mottling caused by overexposure in conjunction with underdevelopment; marks caused by uneven immersion in the developer; marks left on prints that stuck together in the fixer; white fingermarks caused by handling dry photographic paper with damp hands; paper fogged by stray light or an unsafe type of safelight; the flat, grayish appearance of prints made on outdated paper; yellow or brownish stains; and Newton's rings.

Index